DYNAMIC Diva
DOLLARS

For Women Who
Aren't Afraid To Be Millionaires

Elon Bomani

DYNAMIC Diva
DOLLARS

For Women Who Aren't Afraid To Be Millionaires

PAPYRUS PUBLISHING • MISSOURI CITY, TX

This publication is designed to provide accurate and authoritative information in regard to the subject matter covered. It is sold with the understanding that the publisher is not engaged in rendering legal, accounting, or other professional service. If legal advice or other expert assistance is required, please seek the service of a professional person.

Publisher :
Papyrus Publishing
5680 Hwy 6 #166
Missouri City, TX. 77459
281. 394.3384 / Fax :281.394.3390

ISBN: 0-9788288-1-X

Library of Congress Cataloging-In—Publication Data

Bomani, Elon
Dynamic Diva Dollars: For Women Who Aren't Afraid To Become Millionaires
By Elon Bomani.

p.cm.

ISBN: 0-9788288-1-X
1. Finance, Investing
Title: Dynamic Diva Dollars

Printed in the United States of America

Cover Designer: Denise Billups, Borel Graphics
Interior Designer: Pamela Terry, Opus 1 Design

First Printing: 2007

Diva

Acknowledgements

I want to extend my most sincere gratitude to several Divas who have helped me with positive feedback on all of my Diva projects. My best friend and millionaire dream partner, Ms. Mimi Green, her Diva sister, Ms. Valerie Faust. Also, I'd like to extend my sincere appreciation for resources, feedback and support from my Diva confidant, Ms. Akua and my new Diva confidants, Ms. Hicks, and her lovely daughter, Ms. Rhonda Hicks-Smith. Rhonda, you did a great job editing my work. You all inspire me and remind me daily of how truly blessed I am to have such good Diva friends.

No Diva could accomplish such feats without the loving support of her family. First and foremost, I want to thank my Divine husband, Benjamin Harrell for his commitment to this wonderful marriage of ten glorious years and helping raise such lovely boys, Rriiver Nyile and Sirius Seven. I would like to thank, my parents, Warren and Pat Ferebee, who encouraged me in so many ways, but mostly, leading by example. Lastly, but not least, I 'd like to thank my mothers, Dr. Nataki Sunsori and my grandmother, Mildred Ferebee ("the divas") for being the strong rock that I stand on. I am here because of all of you and the ancestors that came before us all.

Diva

CONTENTS

PREFACE   **xiii**

Why This Book?   xvi

Introduction   xxi
    Wealth 101—My Road to Success   xxi
    There Are No Good Paying Jobs Nor SSI   xxiii
    Don't Depend on Your Financial Planner   xxv

How to Use This Book   **xxix**

SECTION I – Dynamic Diva Pre-Wealth Plan   **33**

Dynamic Diva Pre-Wealth Plan   **35**

Develop a Wealth Consciousness   **37**
    Negative Sources   37
    Negative Places   38
    Negative Things and Habits   38
    Negative People   38
    Are You Your Worst Enemy?   39
    Wealth Ways   40
    Wealth Conscious Tools   42

Diva Financial Make-Over   **47**
    Diva Income and Expense Report   48
    Live a Simple Lifestyle by living Below Your Means   48
    Diva's Financial Fast (Elon's Budget Clean up Plan)   49
    Wants vs. Needs List   50
    Don't Play the Shame/Blame Game   51
    K.I.S.S. – Keep it Simple Sister   52

Diva

Create Your Family Financial Statement   **55**
    Savvy Savings Secrets   56
    Five Big Savvy Saving Secrets Tips   58

Credit Card: Good Debts vs. Bad Debts   **63**
    Don't Sweat the Good Debt   64
    Really, How Bad is Credit Card Debt   65
    Credit Card Deletion   67
    Fast Credit Card Debt Pay-Off Plan   68

Great Tax Loopholes   **71**
    Taxes: Uncle Sam Wants Your Money   71

Savings and Retirement   **75**

Estate Planning   **77**

SECTION II – INVESTMENT VEHICLES   **81**

Investment Rules   **83**

Financial Education Investment   **87**

Business Investment – Get Paid Doing What You Love   **89**
    Buy or Create Businesses   89
    Hobby to Profit – Create a Shoe String Business   89
    Network Marketing   90
    Franchises   93
    E-Business   94
    Internet Businesses You Can Easily Learn and Start   96
    Business Plan   102

Real Estate Investment   **105**
    No Money Down Deals   106
    How to Finance Your Real Estate Dreams   109

Diva

Stock Investing   **113**
    Wall Street Wonder women   113
    DRIPs Plan   114
    Hedge Funds   115
    Stock Options   116
    Currency Trading   116
    Commodities Trading   117
    Futures Trading   118
    REITS   119

Bartering Investment   **121**
    Barter: Bargain Trade Secrets   121

Negotiating Investment   **125**
    Negotiate Everything   125

Dynamic Diva Dream Team Investment   **131**

Intellectual Property Investment   **135**
    Get Paid for Your Ideas   135

Networking Investment   **141**

Mentor Investment   **143**

Selling investment   **147**

Giving Investment   **151**

SECTION III – Diva Millionaire Myth   **157**

Diva Millionaire Myth   **157**

**Conscious Capitalist and Socially Responsible
Diva Millionaire**   **161**

Dynamic Diva Wealth Building Plan   **165**

Diva

Dynamic Diva Wealth Builder Plan I (DDWBP I)   166
Dynamic Diva Wealth Builder Plan II   167
Dynamic Diva Wealth Building Prototype,
   "Penny Sense"   168

Final Words   **179**

Diva

Preface

Wealth secrets Colleges, Corporations and Financial Planners Don't Want You to Know

Hi Diva, I am so excited that you have chosen to purchase this book to help you reach your wealth dreams. Imagine having no money worries: Imagine quitting your job and living your dream: not having anymore bills and living debt-free; or being able to buy whatever you want without looking at the price tag. Hard to believe isn't it? Now wait no more. Here in this book lies the simple but many secrets to developing wealth.

I wrote this book because I want you to become rich—very rich! And why not you? It is your birthright to be abundantly successful and wealthy. We live in an abundant world with no limitations. Everyone has an opportunity to life, liberty and happiness. This is what America is all about, right? I am encouraging you to have the courage to take bold steps and defy all odds to reach your full potential, spiritually, and financially.

Most advice given in financial books is antiquated—just plain old and outdated. I have read hundreds of them. The current financial advice offered by most financial planners is too safe, conservative, and foolish. When I hear some of their recommendations, I just want to scream! Most of the information financial planners recommend will have you:

- Debt free, but poor

- Homeless and saving years to buy a home you will be priced out of.

Diva

- Waiting 30 years to retire and hopefully accumulate a million bucks.

Women often start late and cannot *afford*, figuratively and literally, to take their advice any longer. Taxes are going up; the medium price of a nice home is **$250,000** (a quarter of a million dollars) and climbing! How much will it take for you to save the normal down payment of 20% for a $250k home on your meager wages? I'll tell you, $50,000. Twenty-percent of $250,000 is **$50,000**! It cost you **$30,000** for a decent car. Some people would argue that the rate of inflation has increased from 3% to 5%.

With that said, everything is going up, up, up, except for your salary. Salary is too close to the word "slavery" to make me comfortable. Many of you are complaining about "slave wages". You are working harder and longer than what you are getting paid for. To add fuel to the fire, many of you don't like your job anyway. Each day you leave your home singing by the tune, "I owe, I owe, so off to work I go! Why are you there?! I believe you are in the rat race and don't know how to get out of it. I urge you to stop the insanity and read this book to *real* financial freedom. It will teach you how to get out of the rat race to make your own piece of "cheese".

You need to put some things in place that will accelerate your journey on the road to millions. Financial freedom is not free. It comes with a heavy price. You are going to have to take the necessary risk. Financial freedom comes with an inherent risk, but it will be well worth it. I can attest to it. It is time to release your

Diva

fears and anxieties about money and embrace the many wonderful benefits that money can bring into your life, peace of mind being one of them. I can assure you that if you implement some of the information in this book; it will put you on the economic freedom train destined for prosperity promise land. You will be able to accomplish wealth dreams beyond your imagination.

All are welcome aboard the wealth train. Wealth does not discriminate. Most women think it is only for the "good old boys". Wealth does not care if you are young or old, black or white, tall or short, gay or straight, nor male or female. It is readily available to all that seek it with wonder, perseverance and good intentions. There is nothing inherently evil about seeking money. We live in an abundant universe. It is available to each and every one of us who is willing to do the work. Yes, it requires work. But it does not have to be *hard* work. It can be very challenging at times and it will take all of you to master. If any one can master money, Diva you can. Like the old saying goes, *"nothing worthwhile comes easy". If that were the case, then everybody would be doing it.* With *Dynamic Diva Dollars* as your guide, you will learn how to:

- Be debt free and credit rich

- Work smarter with your money instead of harder-learn to do more with less.

- Development a full time or part-time business on a shoe-string budget

- Become house rich

- Retire rich and happy

Diva

WHY THIS BOOK?

It's better to be prepared for a miracle and have one, then to have a miracle and not be prepared

I needed a miracle and I needed it like yesterday! My worst fears had happened. I was in the mist of a break-up with my husband. It was on the same scale as *The War of the Roses*. We had taken our positions. He had his method of defense and I thought I had mine. Like any battle, the main focus was to win the war by any means necessary. He pulled out his major trump card, he emptied "our" joint checking account and transferred "our" income into another account leaving me financially destitute. This was the epitome of emotional and financial abuse. He was the breadwinner and I was the dependent stay-at-home mom—or so he thought.

In order to save my soul and my sanity, my spirit said it was time to go-right now! I got the hell out of there! In a matter of minutes, my child and I were poor and homeless.
Diva, I had to think fast. This was no time to panic. This was a time to pray. The Dynamic Diva within me was born again. I had turned into the lioness that was determined to protect her cub. My spirit instructed me to use my credit card to stay at a hotel. After a restless night, the next morning I used the yellow pages, and called a local woman's shelter. They usually do not take women unless they were being physically abused. But with the Divine spirit on my side, I told her I was desperate and staying at a hotel with my child, and she kindly let me come. I will always be grateful to Maat and the Placer County Women Center.

Diva

With all the spiritual work I had done over the years, I was very clear that this was not about "What my husband did to me". It was about what I was thinking and doing to myself. I had to realize it was not my husband who got me in the predicament that I was in, it was about what I was thinking and doing to myself that bought me to that point in my life. The drama queen in me was healed; I was willing to take full responsibility for where I was at in my life. My husband had to deal with his karma, and that was none of my business. What was my business was to figure out how I let this happen! I thought I was an independent, strong powerful woman of the new millennium-with a college degree. How could I be in such a predicament if that were the case. I had to dig deep to uncover some negative unconscious issues about myself—and quickly.

Introspection during a deep meditation revealed to me some startling truths. My father had left my mother and she was forced to take care of my sister and me alone. My fear was that my husband would do the same to me. So, I created circumstances to bring my self-fulfilled prophecy to light. Like my mother, I would be a single woman who would have to raise my child alone. Thoughts are very powerful, they create your reality. There will be more on this subject later.

Like many women, two weeks after having my baby, I returned to work to run my naturopathic private practice with my baby in tow. I tried everything to make it work. It didn't. I had to make a decision. Should I let someone else raise my child or give up my practice and become a stay-at-home mom? The decision was easy. I could always reopen another practice,

Diva

but I could not miss out on the once in a life time moments of growing and bonding with my bundle of joy. So, I closed my practice and became a stay- at-home mom.

I was conditioned by society that money issues and business affairs were handled by men. Though I successfully passed several math and science classes, I still believed I was too inadequate to handle matters of money and nonchalantly passed on the management of my business financial matters to my husband. As well, my husband was in charge of the financial purse strings at home. I was a great healer but not a savvy business woman.

Eureka! I got the spiritual message. As a Holistic practitioner, I was out of balance financially. If you are unbalanced in one area of your life it will have an adverse effect in other areas of your life-spiritually, physically, and emotionally. I had to get my financial act together for me and my son.

I took charge of my financial life and a blessing has happened! I get to stay at home with my baby and still make a substantial income. I studied the power of money and as a result money and I became friends. In less than one year, I acquired 1.5 million dollars worth of real estate, bought a house, a car and accomplished my dream of raising a healthy prosperous child while working from home! Not a bad start from someone who started with just $36 dollars in her checking account. I became my own financial expert and via this book I want to encourage you to become your own financial expert, too.

I will share this journey and show how I started out financially illiterate and poor and became financial educated and

Diva

free. My story will help you understand why you may have not accomplished your wealth dreams, if you truly recognize your Diva power, you will become excited and implement changes in your life to become a Dynamic Diva with Dollars.

Nina

Diva

Introduction

Wealth 101—My Road to Success

Like many of you *still* think, I thought a college education, good government and a corporate job coupled with a financial planner would create my ticket to financial freedom. Having gone to a top university and investing thousands of dollars, I was sure that a four year degree would guarantee me a piece of the American Dream:

- A great paying job

- A comfortable lifestyle: nice house, car, married with 2.5 kids and yearly vacations

- An affluent retirement

I set myself up for a rude awakening. My life after college was not going in a prosperous direction. I automatically believed that a better education would give me a better life. I was not living the American dream, I was living the American nightmare of the working poor living pay check to pay check, up to my ears in debt; with barely enough for the basic necessities of life-food, a decent car, clothing and shelter. I was in the rat race and I did not know how to break the vicious cycle of poverty. My salary was not the problem. It was what I was doing and not doing with my money that put me in financial peril.

In hindsight, I realized when I was paid a decent salary; I was clueless as to what to do with the money I was making. To my dismay, I was *financially illiterate*! After 18 years of so-called

Diva

formal and higher education, I did not understand *anything* about money! The 3R's proved not to be enough for me and most Americans. The educational system is in desperate need of an educational make-over. Financial education needs to be a part of the curriculum and a required course-starting at the pre-school level.

I thought a college education was supposed to prepare me for life. Isn't one of life's major necessities **M-O-N-E-Y?!** It is right up there with oxygen. The truth of the matter is that college is designed to *train* you to get a job. To put it succinctly, the acronym for J-O-B is "Just Over Broke"! **A J-O-B IS CREATED BY THE OWNER OF THE BUSINESS TO HAVE YOU WORK FOR HIM SO THAT HE CAN BECOME WEALTHY AND RETIRE ON THE BEACH-NOT YOU.** As long as you have a job, you are securing someone else's financial future.

Did you know some of the wealthiest people in the world have become wealthy without a college degree? Yes, Bill Gates and Michael Dell, just to name a few, are college drop-outs! College does not encourage innovative new ideas, it encourages the status quo.

The best example of this fact is the story of Fred Smith, the founder of Federal Express. While at Yale University, Mr. Smith received a C on the paper he wrote about an idea to create a next day mail delivery service. His professor did not believe someone would pay such a high price for mail. As you may know now the world cannot live without Federal Express and it was made better because of one man's idea and determination

Diva

to prove his critics wrong. He took an idea that was a place in his *heart,* listened to his *gut feeling* and made it a reality.

My lack of financial education made me poor, pitiful and pissed-off. I knew if I wanted my life to change, I was going to have to take responsibility for my financial circumstance and focus on changing it for the better. I went on a personal quest to master money before money mastered me. I had to do what my college did not do for me----create my own personalized wealth university.

I named my first class Wealth 101 and now I am a lifetime student of it. Education is derived from the Latin word *educe* which means to draw out. A financial education is designed to draw out the natural money savvy abilities within you. Divas, you already have what it takes to fulfill your wildest financial dreams. Now all you need to do is **pay attention** and go within. Congratulations!

There are no good paying jobs nor SSI
Another major reason why I decided to create my own wealth university is because the government no longer intends to support my retirement. I know that social security is not going to be around when I reach retirement. My retirement money is being used right now to assist the people who are retired today. Even if I were to receive a retirement check from SSI, with the rate of inflation, it would not be enough to live on. I, like many others, would be forced to work at the golden arches during my golden years. Can you imagine a Diva working at Mickey D's with teenagers? I shutter at the thought!

Diva

When I looked at good government and corporate job opportunities, it became very clear that they were not hiring permanent employees because they would have to provide benefits and a pension plan. Additionally, many companies and government institutions are no longer offering defined-benefit plans. To make matter worst, the government is letting corporate companies and government institutions off the hook from paying pension plans to their employees.

United Airlines by a court ruling was allowed to claim bankruptcy and stop the payment of their pension plan to their employees who have worked 20 to 30 years. This left one pilot in California very upset. He was anticipating receiving a retirement plan in 2 years of $12,000.00 per month. Now, it is projected he will receive around $2,400.00 per month. It became clear to me that the government was no longer going to protect or take responsibility for my retirement.

Lastly, as I started to do my own wealth building homework, I came upon many financial planners who wanted to give me advice as to what to do with my money. One top company advisor wanted me to pay $695.00 for a financial analysis and take a large percentage of my profit if I chose his investment package. As I looked at him across the table my *first thought* was how a man with a job can teach me how to become wealthy when he is not wealthy himself. According to his plan, it would take 30 years to become a millionaire and I could not afford to wait that long to make my first million. Moreover, I remember a joke that holds some truth: the reason why they call them stockbrokers is because they are always broke. They

Diva

get paid commission dollars that impede the chances of your stocks growing.

Don't Depend on Your Financial Planner

It is financial suicide to depend, solely, on your financial planner to take care of your money. I don't dislike financial planners, I was a licensed and registered representative and I enjoyed helping people with their investment goals. I think there are many who serve their clients well. On the other hand, there are many more that provide poor service, losing a lot of their client's money. I think now the status quo advice of doing dollar cost averaging, investing in diversified mutual funds, buying low, selling high, does not apply to our current economy. I discovered that financial planners know as much about stock as you and I do. Too many rely on historical precedence. I think we are in a time and age that the way of investing and investment vehicles have changed. Depending on financial planners to take care of your money is not the way to accumulate wealth.

In essence, depending on the educational institutions, your government/corporate job or your financial planner to help you acquire wealth is not wise. These venues serve the five percent who control the world resources, not you. As long as their agenda is not your agenda, you will have to take responsibility for determining you financial future.

After doing some real soul searching and introspections, I came to the startling conclusion that I had given my power away. I allowed myself to be programmed and conditioned to believed that I needed someone else (the so-called experts) to

Diva

make my financial decisions. I was broke because of the dis-
empowering position that I had put myself in. I had only one
alternative to choose in order to get my financial life back on
track. I had to take control of my bad money habits and establish good money habits. The end result is this book that I have
written for you so that you can do the same.

The methods presented to you are short and concise. This
book is a brief how-to, self- help vehicle. It is by no means
the be all and end all book. Matter of fact, I recommend that
you read more books, go to conference/seminars about wealth
building and search the internet for a plethora of financial information. Keep in contact with me at *www.thedynamicdiva.*
com and I will have all the up-to-date information on all of
your health, wealth and spiritual needs. Do not forget to sign
up for your free e-zine.

Why am I so confident that these methods work? It made me
a self-made millionaire in two short years! This is the fool-proof
method I used that allowed me to escape the rat race, build a
financial portfolio that allowed me to retire at 39 and be a stay -
at- home Mom. I am blessed to be living my wealth dream. Keep
in mind, I started out with no job; I was homeless with a two
year old baby; $36 dollars in my checking account and a dream
when I brought my first house. I do not tell you this information
to impress you, but to impress upon you that if I can do it, you
can do it too! You have access to the same resources as I have.
And some of you are in a better place in your life than I was
when I got started. This book is a guide to get you started with
the major focus on areas that have worked for me.

Diva

DIVA TIP: As I write this book the rules about money are changing every millisecond. You must keep yourself abreast of what is going on. Wealth is a life time educational journey. The more you study and implement wealth ideas in your life, the greater chance you will have of reaching your financial goals. Choose to be a life time wealth builder and you will be rewarded with riches. If you believe as I do that each one should teach one, pass this information along to someone else you want to help in life. Buy this book for a friend or family member or direct them to my website *www.thedynamicdiva.com* for a free e-zine so they, too, can become wealthy. I am so happy at where my life is right now and I want to share it with my friends so we all can be happy and financially free. I know it will make for a better world when we have more Divas at peace than stressed out, living in the rat race. There is plenty of money for everyone in the world to live an abundant life. Do not believe that there is not enough money to go around. It is love that makes the world go round and round and money is a reflection of how much love we have to give. I love you.

Peace and Prosperity to you,

Elon Bomani
The Dynamic Diva
www.thedynamicdiva.com
Inspiring women to become more healthy, wealthy and wise

Nina

Diva

How to Use This Book

Divas, I recommend you read the entire book first before you start to do the work. Once you read it then put to use Section One – Section Three in that order. You should read the **DIVA TIPS** for great advice and resources you can investigate to further your education about investments or wealth information I have shared with you.

Section One: The Pre-Wealth Building Plan

This section of the book focuses on organizing your finances. It outlines basic steps Divas can take in order to develop a good relationship with money and incorporate good money habits. Once you have established a good solid financial foundation, you will be ready to invest.

Section Two: Dynamic Diva Investments Guide

This is a cornucopia of investment vehicles that Divas can study to help build their personalized wealth portfolio. The goal of this section is to expose you to the many conventional and unconventional investment vehicles you can use to help you reach your financial goals. The conventional investment vehicles are real estate, businesses and the stock market. The unconventional investment vehicles are financial education, negotiating and bartering-just to name a few. All are mentioned because I think that these are the best vehicles that will help to make and save you money. Moreover, if you use them all well, you should get a return on your investment

Diva

20% or above.

This section will explain the investment vehicles and provide suggested resources Divas can investigate to develop greater knowledge of the subject. I suggest you read all of the investment options and pick the ones that peak your interest and determine which works well with your investment personality.

Section Three: Dynamic Diva Wealth Building Plan

This section will give you examples of two plans you can implement to help you reach financial security. The idea is that once you are financially secure, you can focus your energy on building wealth. The Dynamic Diva Wealth Builder Plan I is for Divas who want to get wealthy quickly. The Dynamic Diva II plan is for Diva who wants to take the tortoise approach and start on a part-time basis.

"Penny Sense" is an outline of how a Diva, a fictitious character, uses The Dynamic Diva Wealth Building Plan I to help her become financially free. "Penny Sense" is an example of how your financial plan could look if you take action.

Once again, read the book in its entirety and do the work right away. Do not delay, wealth can be yours starting today!

Diva

Section I

Dynamic Diva Pre-Wealth Plan

Diva

Dynamic Diva
Pre-Wealth Plan

iva, you do have your work cut out for you if you are starting from ground zero to reach your goal of becoming a Dynamic Diva Millionaire. Hey, but you are a Diva. Divas relish the opportunity to shine in the light of the most formidable task. This is the time for you to take charge of your financial life and get a clear understanding of where exactly you are money wise and how far you want to go to be financially free.

There is a system to wealth building and the Dynamic Diva Dollars Pre-Wealth Building Plan is strategically designed to get you there a lot quicker than myself. I have eliminated what did not work for me and incorporated what did help me reach my level of success. By following this plan, you will minimize your level of mistakes and save time and money. Most important, this plan will take out the guess work to riches and hasten your quick rise to financial freedom. Take these actions today to keep poverty away.

This section will provide you with the necessary steps you must take in order to set a good, strong financial foundation that will help accelerate your efforts to becoming a millionaire. This list of task is arranged in the exact order you should follow for best results. There is no better place to start than at the beginning.

Develop a Wealth Consciousness

"Whether you realize it or not, your level of wealth and success reflects exactly what you believe you deserve"
Louise L. Hay

iva, before we can discuss developing a wealthy conscious, let's analyze and get a handle on some of the most pervasive dream killers that plague you on a daily basis. You must avoid at all cost, negative sources, people, place, things and habits.

Negative Sources

One negative source that has a profound effect on us on a daily basis is the media. The majority of television, radio, newspaper, internet and other media outlets are made up of negative information that keep you in a perpetual state of fear. You are bombarded by information that states you can only find happiness if you have this car, wear these clothes, and buy this great vacation package. You get my point? I, highly recommend, you decrease significantly or eliminate these negative sources of entertainment and information. Another option, go on a media fast! Choose a certain amount of time you will go without any media contact. I do it often. I watch minimal television or news of any kind. I, honestly, am having too much fun creating my wealth dreams, like writing this book. Instead, utilize your time away from the media to focus on creating your dreams.

Negative Places

Most often if you go to the casino, you will spend money gambling; if you are in a bar, you will drink; and if you are entertaining your drama queen friends, you will bring more drama into your life. Conversely, if you are in the gym, you will workout; if you attend a wealth building workshop, you will build wealth; and if you are a part of a book club, you will network with people of like mind and read great books. Your environment plays a major role in the type of experiences you have. Look at the places you frequent and ask yourself is this a positive place that make me feel comfortable. If not, leave. people

Negative Things and Habits

Negative things and habits seem to go hand in hand. Most of the things we do daily become habits. It has become such a part of our routine that we do not realize the negative side effects of our actions. What we want to do is eliminate the things that have become bad habits and replace them with good habits; for example, gossiping, shopping, eating and drinking too much just to name a few. Instead, learn to spend your time developing new productive habits like walking daily, reading good books or trying a new hobby. Have you noticed that all of these negative habits cost money and lots of it. You can kill two birds with one stone here. If you eliminate the negative habits, you can save money too.

Negative People

Another "Neg" is negative people. Negative people are dream killers. They give you unsolicited negative advice. They are the first to tell you what you cannot do rather than what you can do- the naysayer. They are very pessimistic about everything and they tend to drain you energy. Unfortunately, the majority of negative people you come into contact with live in your house.

Choose not to give your power away. The best way to deal with negative people is to limit your contact with them. Do not tell them anything about your dreams. Like Iyanla Vanzant stated, "Do not let them breath on you baby". Keep your most important dreams to yourself and only share the intimate details with God (very dependable and supportive) and the positive people you know. If all else fails release negative toxic people from your life. Sometime you are going to be the one who has to leave in order to see a positive change. But keep in mind, as one door closes, another door of equal or greater benefit will open.

Are You Your Worst Enemy?

Divas, you are a person too. Are you your worst enemy? If you are having difficulties with your money, it is important that you now take the time to make a concerted effort to unearth your core beliefs about money. Do you have a love/hate relationship with money? If so, at what point in your life was it created?

Most fears about money start during early childhood. We either adopted positive or negative attitudes and habits about money from our family. Was money hard to come by? Did your family barely make ends meet? Or did you have lots of money and spent it when you made it? Even worst, did you grow up without a care about money because it was one topic that you never discussed with your family? One thing is very clear, if you started life with poor money habits, you will only carry over those same habits into your adult life.

If today you find that your conversations about money are negative, you have developed a negative consciousness about money. How often are you saying things like, "He is filthy rich", "Money is the root of all evil", "I have to rob Peter to pay Paul and "Money won't buy you happiness"? The list goes on and on. Where you are right now, you put yourself there. If you have a negative attitude, you will draw to you negative experiences. Most negative people are angry, jealous, and envious individuals. They have an inability to forgive. If they have a negative experience, it is always the other person's fault. A person with a negative attitude plays the victim/blame game. And a person with a severe case of the "Negs" is a Drama King or Queen. They always have a tragic story to tell. Be honest with yourself, does any of this sound like you?

If these sounds like you, here are some techniques you can use to get rid of the "Negs". Decide to be a positive person and develop a positive attitude. Forgive yourself and everyone in your life that has caused you pain. Choose to release anger, jealousy and envy from your life. Realize that you are the controller of your destiny and no one can make you feel or act negatively without your consent. Make the decision not to create drama in you life any more. And when drama show up looking like "Crazy", immediately turn in the opposite direction and run. Get out! Struggle is optional and you can choose to look at the bright side of everything going on in your life.

Wealthy Ways

If you are willing to acknowledge and take responsibility for your actions, you will be able to develop the power to release what is not working for you. Make a valiant effort to think positively, speak positively and associate with positive people.

By doing so, you will manifest a positive outcome. It truly is that simple. Refer to my complimentary book *Wealth Chants-Chanting your way to an abundant lifestyle* for further support.

If money has been elusive and difficult to acquire in your life, I encourage you to begin to use proactive, practical techniques to help deprogram your mind of negative consciousness toward money and encourage more positive images of money and your relationship with money. These techniques helped me make the transition from not being on speaking terms with money and becoming best friends with money. I had to, literally, pray, meditate, visualize and talk myself into becoming wealthy. Now, I love money and money loves me. We get along very well and my financial statement show the positive results from making a conscious shift from negative beliefs about money to more positive beliefs about money.

Wealth is the idea of having more than enough. It is an abundance of tangible and intangible assets. You can have a wealth of health, a wealth of knowledge and a wealth of material goods. Accumulating wealth in one area of your life has a domino effect of creating wealth in all other areas of your life according to the law of cause and effect. In other words, within you are all the resources you need, mental, emotional, physical and spiritual to manifest worth in your life. Wealth is not something that happens to a few "lucky" people. Lucky people win the lottery and two years later claim bankruptcy because they were not mentally prepared to handle the fortune. True wealth can only be obtained if you make a concerted effort to condition your mind to dramatically shift from negative feelings of worthlessness and lack to more positive feelings of self-worth and abundance. Now you are ready to implement the wealth conscious tools that will help you developing a prosperous mindset.

WEALTH CONSCIOUSNESS TOOLS

Create a "Peace Place"

Dedicate a room in your home or space in the corner of a room to do your wealth conscious work. You can prepare a prosperity altar. The prosperity altar is your place where you can get the inspiration from your divine source to help you accomplish you wealth dreams. This is the place were you **pray, meditate, affirm, visualize** and **Yoga** your way to abundance. At your altar, you want to place things that will inspire you like books and picture of wealthy individuals you admire. Make sure the five elements are represented: earth, air, water, fire, and ether. Here are some items that best represent the five elements, candles, incense, flowers, crystals, small bowl of water, a plant, and a picture of an ancestor or angel. In the end, use your intuition and imagination to create your own unique prosperity altar.

Pray

Prayer allows one to commune with God. Ask for divine guidance for assistance on building prosperity in your life the righteous way. When you pray to the source of all good, grace and mercy is bound to reign.

Meditate

Meditation allows the spirit within us to speak and wisely guide you to fulfill your divine purpose on this earth. This is the place where our truth lies. Meditation gives us back our quiet time and the ability to think. It's such a busy world. The ability to listen and think with our inner voice has become a luxury. In that quiet space, divine messages will greet you and clear out noisy chatter to make room for your divinely inspired wealth dreams.

Affirm

Affirmations give you the opportunity to speak truth into your life. You can confirm the positive in the here and now. What you say sends off a vibration into the universe to bring it back to you. So, you are put on notice to watch your words and respect its power. For example, how many times have you said I am broke and money has been difficult to find. Now affirm, I have more than enough money available to me. For a greater understanding of this subject read my book, *Wealthy Chants: Chanting your way to an abundant lifestyle*

Wealth Chant

Chanting is the ability to repeat words in succession. This ancient art is believed to evoke an energetic force within the mind that extends throughout the body to encourage the physical manifestation of the words. By you chanting words of abundance or wealth, you will create an atmosphere of prosperity coming into your life. Once the prosperous condition make its presence known (aka divine intervention), you must take immediate action to bring to existence the wealth experience. For example, one day my wealth chant was "my income is increasing daily". Upon completing this simple exercise, I got the inspiration to write and publish my first book about money, *Wealthy Chants*. Many wonderful wealth chants came to mind. There was no writer's block and I am creating a new business as a publisher/author to increase my income potential.

Diva tip: Go to my website *www.thedynamicdiva.com* for the Daily Inspiration of the day and sign up for my free e-zine for more great money tips.

Visualize

Visualization is the act of mentally creating the outcome of any situation you aspire. It is the act of seeing the thing with the minds eye first and directing the body to respond to the vision. Hence, if you want to create a successful business, you must see yourself successfully going through all the necessary motion to bring that act to fruition. By mentally creating the act with the mind, the body will act accordingly. This is truly an act of mind over matter.

Yoga

The philosophy of yoga is to establish union between the mind and the body. This union brings balance and harmony into your life which makes way for the creative spirit to emanate from within. The physical act of yoga is a wonderful exercise that conditions and tones the body's organs and balance the chakra (the energy forces in the body that allows you to align with the spirit).

Journal

Journal your thoughts. The transcriptions bring your words into the physical realm and make them real and tangible. You are putting yourself and the universe on notice that you are ready to take the necessary steps to bring your wealth dreams into reality in the here and now. Additionally, keeping a journal will help to organize your thoughts and allow you to monitor how well you are progressing. This is the point where action begins.

Diva Tip: You should try to practice using these wealth consciousness tools for 21 days consecutively. By then, they should become a habit and you would have developed a wealthy conscious. At this time, you should create your Dynamic Diva Dream Plan of (1) immediate (1 yr.), (2) intermediate (3-5yrs.), and (3) long term financial dreams (5-10yrs.), you want to accomplish. When making your Dynamic Diva Dream Financial Plans, be specific, clear and dream Big-dreams, the impossible dream.

DIVA TIP II: For your *free* downloadable Dynamic Diva Financial Plan worksheet, go to *www.thedynamicdiva.com/worksheets. html*

DIVA TIP III: Need more wealth conscious tools, check out this great e-book, *http://imdiva.vitale.hop.clickbank.net/*

Diva Financial Make-Over

Divas, first, you have to take a long good look at your financial situation. It is time for you to be brutally honest with yourself about all of your money matters. Are you living below or above your means? Do you have a budget, and if you do, is it in the negative each month? Is your debt high or low? How much money do you have in your savings account? Do you have a savings account? How much money can you live on a year comfortably without going to work? If you do not know the answers to each of these questions, you need to start at the beginning. If you do, you need to reevaluate and change some aspect of it in order to accommodate your new lifestyle goals. No matter if you are a stay-at-home mom, professional woman or a wanna-be at home mom still working in corporate America, you can begin to organize you finances so that you can find the income to allow you to stay at home or create the career that you were destined to do. You need to begin with a Diva Financial Statement, a Diva Income and Expense Report and, last but not least, a Diva Dream Plan.

DIVA TIP: You can find the Diva Financial Statement, Diva Income and Expense Report and the Diva Dream Plan *free* downloadable at *www.thedynamicdiva.com/worksheets.html.*

DIVA INCOME AND EXPENSE REPORT

The Diva income and expense report is made up of income, money you bring home from your job, monthly passive income, child support and other revenue sources. Put succinctly, income is all incoming funds. Expenses are bills you have to pay on a monthly basis like the utility bills, mortgage, alimony, insurance, etc. This is all out going funds. Once you have your determined your present budget, now we will focus on how we can take that budget and create a new spending plan.

Live a Simple Lifestyle by living Below Your Means

Divas can do this. Divas have been living below their means since the beginning of time. Unlike many men, divas are more inclined to understand that our net worth does not determine our self-worth. We are the Queens of making sacrifices and doing without for the sake of our family. So this may come natural for you. I mean really, how much money do you need to live on yearly to be comfortable.

Most of us think we do not have any spare change once we complete the Diva Income and Expense Report. We think we need a lot of things that are in our budget in order to live a happy life. I know for myself when I truly looked at my budget and got real serious about wanting to stay at home. I tried to find every cost cutting technique in existence. I was surprised to find out when I cut my cost I had more than enough to live off of and I began to have fun thinking about various choices that I had to utilize my money. Money was no longer controlling

48

me, I was finally controlling my money and I felt empowered and not at the mercy of society and family as to what a happy life was. I was carving out my own financial niche to live by: This is what I did and I am sure many of you women have a lot of these costly events in your life. Let them go, and you to will find the additional funds within the money you and your family are making to help you stay at home. Or, it will get you closer to setting more realistic money choices. Just like when we make a mess in the house, we need to now focus on cleaning up the financial mess we make in our life. Below you will find my budget clean up plan (also known as Diva's Financial Fast). What is yours?

Diva's Financial Fast (Elon's Budget Clean up Plan)

1. Eliminated getting my hair done- ($100.00 /mo.)

2. No more daily stops at Jamba Juice- ($3.75 x 20 = $75.00/ mo.)

3. Manicures/pedicures- ($40.00/mo.)

4. Stick to a food budget, no buying snack on the spur of the moment ($50.00/mo.)

5. Stop eating out ($250.00/mo.)

6. No more miscellaneous items-lotion, make-up, paper towels, tissues etc. ($50.00/mo.)

7. Fasted once a week- for spiritual, health and financial reasons $(25.00)

8. No more dry cleaning ($20.00/mo.)

9. No clothes shopping (100.00/mo.)

10. Did my laundry once a week and before 7am and after 7pm

11. Learn energy saving tips for the house ($50.00/mo.)

12. Bought phone service unlimited plan ($100.00/mo.)

13. Eliminated all cable channels- was not good programming anyway ($40.00/mo.)

14. Eliminated DSL ($50.00/mo.)

15. Never bought a cell phone- even though all my peers tried to pressure me about it.

16. Reunited with my husband- divorce is very costly. You have to start all over again

17. Reduced my home and auto insurance ($300.00/mo.)

18. Refinanced my house ($500.00/mo.)

19. Sold my SUV car and downsized to a modest station wagon - created less cost for auto insurance, monthly gas, yearly registration and auto repair. **Major Savings!** **($250.00/mo.)**

20. No big vacations- more bonding and intimate relationship with the ones I love.

21. No or dramatically minimized gift giving during the holiday season- this is another big money saver. ($50.00/mo.)

I was able to save $2050.00 per month - which is almost a full salary. The Diva Financial Fast helped me to stay at home and create funds to invest. By doing a financial fast and scaling back on your expenditures, I am sure you will be able to find the necessary funds to help you achieve your personal wealth goals.

Wants vs. Needs List

How much money can you and your family live on comfortably each year? What is the yearly income needed to maintain a basic simple lifestyle? There are some basic things we need in order to function well. We need food, shelter, and clothing. You may feel that transportation, entertainment funds and an insurance policy etc. are a necessity. You may want to include a vacation. You need to get your hair done monthly. The key words are truly deciding the difference between what you *want* and what you *need.*

Needs are things you cannot function without. They are things that will dramatically affect the well-being of your life. Wants are desire we aspire but we can live without. Make a list of what you absolutely need in your life that your family depends on for survival and a list of what you want. Once you decipher between your wants and your needs, it is now time to develop a **New Dynamic Diva spending plan** that will help you *choose* who you will share your money with.

Diva Tip: You can create your own Needs vs. Wants List or go to *www.thedynamicdiva.com/worksheets.html* for your free downloadable Needs vs. Wants list and New Dynamic Diva Spending Plan list.

Don't Play the Shame/Blame Game

As you begin to look at your money issues and start to prepare your spending plan, feelings of regret will start to surface. This is not the time or goal to be ashamed of your past money management snafus. Nor is it a time to feel guilty about the college fund you have yet to start for your child that is now in her teens. Yes, it is time to admit you are learning strong money lessons. What needs to happen at this time is to discern the truth about what is working in your money world and discard what is not working. Be open and free with this information without attaching yourself to an outcome that you feel forces you to make a right or wrong decision today. It is more important to process the information without being judgmental about it. It is okay to critique your passed actions regarding money, but is not okay to criticize your action.

Please honor and support yourself through this process. Focus on what you want to happen in your life with money. And give power only to that. You and I have wasted precious time on blaming the politicians, the I.R.S. and the phone company - by the way, who made those calls- adding to our financial woes. You now know after some self-reflection that if your relationship with money is going to change for the positive, you are going to have to shift your consciousness dramatically. More importantly, you will have to take action right away by implementing the plans or suggestions in this book that will bring about the change. Do the work, now!!!!!!!!!!!!

K.I.S.S. - Keeping it Simple, Sister

If we all are really honest with ourselves, we get most of our joy out of life when we live a simple lifestyle: waking up early to watch the sunrise, eating wholesome natural simple foods, spending quality time with the family in the park feeding the ducks, wearing comfortable clothes that allow our body to breathe. You could write a letter to a dear friend you haven't spoken to in awhile. Praying over dinner with the family and discussing our daily activities can be enjoyable. And we can volunteer our time for a local community charity. All of these enjoyable and fulfilling acts do not cost a lot of money- many are free- but bring to our hearts wealth of peace and tranquility that is priceless. It makes our life feel "rich" and fulfilling.

I can remember when I was a little child thinking that I came from a wealthy family supported by my single-mom. We had everything my heart desired- a loving happy home. We never wanted for clothes or a meal. We played. We studied hard and got a good education. And occasionally, we went to McDonalds or played miniature golf with the family. What more could one want. Little did I know that we were poor and supported by public assistance.

Even so, we did not let our financial circumstances dictate our attitude about life. Ironically, when we improved our economic status to middle class and started living like "the Jones" our quality of life took a downturn and became more complex. We had all the trapping of success- cars, homes, vacations, dining out regularly- but we did not have each other.

Society had convinced us that the true show of wealth is the accumulation of a lot of material things—and we *bought* into it only to realize that it made us spiritually and emotionally destitute.

Divas, lets choose to return to the simple way of life by creating a new spending plan that will be reflective of it. You will find it to be personally gratifying and save you a ton of money because we know that buying more make-up and clothes is not going to bring you more peace of mind nor improve you quality of life. It will only have you worrying about your next credit card bill and an empty savings account.

Nina

Create Your
Family Financial Statement

A financial statement is a report that shows the financial condition of a person. A financial statement is quite easy to do. First, you write down all of your assets. Assets are financial resources that you have possession of now. An asset can be liquid or non-liquid. A liquid asset is cash that you can easily get assess to. For example, a liquid asset is money in your checking, savings, money market account or stock account which you can retrieve on a moments notice. On the other hand, non-liquid asset can be real estate, land, business or merchandise you can only get cash from once you sell it. Unfortunately, selling these types of assets takes time and for that reason the money is not easily available to you.

The second step requires you to record your liabilities. These are debts that you owe. Liabilities include mortgages, credit card debts, car loans etc. And on the third step, you take your total assets and minus your total debts and the final answer will be your net worth. Your net worth is a true indicator of how much money and valuables you have acquired.

DIVA TIP: For a free downloadable copy of a Diva Financial Statement go to *www.thedynamicdiva.com*

Savvy Saving Secrets

Once you have prepared your Dynamic Dream Plan, Diva Income and Expense Report, Diva Financial Statement, determine your Want Vs. Needs, you are now ready to create your New Diva Spending Plan, you will be able to see where your money is going. You can now take the 3 % from your savings column and put it away in a money market account for a rainy or sunny day to serve as an emergency fund.

I know you may not be able to go cold turkey, but this is a major financial diet you may have to go on. Even so, you can start by cutting down on some of the items from your want list. You will notice more dollars in your pocket.

Divas tend to be more frugal with the dollar. This is a great thing. You are probably saying to yourself right now, "I do not have any money to save, once I pay all the bills". I beg to differ. If you have done your Diva Income and Expense Report, Diva Financial Fast and adhered to your Wants vs. Needs List, you should be able to create a spending plan that will produce discretionary funds-money you can save for a sunny day.

Occasionally, you have heard good advice from various financial gurus when they recommend paying yourself first. This is very important for financial reasons as well as psychological reasons.

Psychologically, when you pay yourself first, you are acknowledging that money is here to serve you. You are honoring you by making you your first priority. For Divas, it is very important that we develop a relationship with money that allows us to experience the joy of it by allowing it to take care of our desires. Divas tend to see money as a means of taking care of everybody else- the bill collectors, the kids, and our family. Using money as a means of making sacrifices only, will have you looking at money as the sacrificial lamb instead of the abundance builder it was destined to be.

You must get serious about savings because it will help you create an emergency fund, that will decrease the stress from the unexpected things that enter our lives- hospital bill, automobile repairs, family emergency etc. Moreover, you can take the savings and put it in an investment vehicle that will give you a greater return for your money rather than a typical savings account at your local bank. This will take the stress away from worrying about future money problems because they will not exist with adequate savings. Most important, this will increase your confidence in your ability to be responsible with money by utilizing it more wisely.

The financial gurus also recommend that you pay yourself 10% of your monthly income. Obviously, many of these gurus are not Divas because that is very steep when you have a family. So, I recommend you save 3% of your monthly income. This should be possible for even the financially strapped. Moreover, you can take action today to get those savings together that will allow you to stay at home.

Here is a great example. Let's say Vanessa makes $2500.00 per month. Three percent of $2500.00 dollars would allow her to save 75.00 per month. Vanessa major want was getting her hair done twice a month for $100.00. She decided to take that out of her spending plan and convert $75.00 to a saving plan that will net her 2% interest from the bank for borrowing her money. Now her money is making more money for her. Exciting! If she saves $75 for one year, she will have $900.00 dollars. She is on her way.

DIVA TIP: Three percent is a very low savings goal but it is feasible for beginning Diva wealth builders. But the goal is to graduate to saving 10% and eventually to 30% of your income towards your savings and/or investments on a monthly basis. The more you save and invest, the quicker you will reach your goal to millions.

DIVA TIP II: If you still think you cannot find the extra funds, you may be a little resistant to the idea of building wealth. This is the time to sit and meditate on ways you can control your money before your money starts to control you.

FIVE BIG SAVVY SAVING SECRETS

1. Shelter

Buy a home – It may cost you less than renting at the end of the year because you maybe able to write off the mortgage interest. The house can build equity over the years since most properties appreciate 5 to 6 percent annually. In other words, homeownership can save and make you money.

Also, if you cannot afford to buy a home or do not want to buy a home, consider lease option to buy. First, it allows you to possibly own a home even if you have bad credit, no money for a down payment or no closing cost for a home. It will allow you to lock in the price in the year you lease option and save you money in the long run.

Another real estate option is to purchase a home in foreclosure or Real Estate Owned (REO) and buy it at 70% below market value. There are plenty of deals out there. Try to never buy a home at retail. Buy a home at wholesale. This will give you a home with built in equity which will be of great value to you if you want to pull out cash to invest in other investments in the future.

2. Clothing

Buy clothes when they are on sale and going out of season. For example, buy winter clothes in the end of winter and summer at the end of summer. The prices are usually sliced in half. Never buy clothes on impulse or because it is on sale. When you go shopping for clothes have a list of the items and only get what is on the list. The worst thing to do is to buy two shirts because it is 50% off the second one when you had on the list to buy only one. You must stay within the budget. If your clothing allowance is $50 for the month, do not spend a penny more.

Stop wearing somebody's name on your shirt and jeans. You pay about 30% more for an item for the privilege of wearing a designer's name. Leave the expensive department stores and shop at Wal-Mart or the outlets. They have great bargains that are cheap but still made of good quality and great prices. You will save tremendously.

If you must have the designer brands, shop at consignment stores. Wealthy people change their wardrobe yearly and get rid of some expensive name brand clothes.

Also, you can shop thrift or second hand store for some great deals and create your own style. The clothes do not make the Diva but the Diva make the clothes.

3. Food

Divas, can you say coupons? Start cutting out coupons that pertain to the foods you normally eat. Do not buy the food just because you have a coupon for it, especially if you do not normally eat it. Verify the real value of the coupon. Many coupons are made by a company to get the item moving but are not really a deal. Generic items are sometimes better than coupons because they are cheaper and usually are made by the famous name brands but are marketed by the supermarket store. It is also a good idea to shop at the bulk supermarket store because the prices are cheaper.

Try eating a vegetarian diet. Meats are very expensive. Buy more economical foods like beans and rice. They are healthier for you. If you eat a vegetarian diet in the long run you will save medical bills because vegetarians are less prone to diseases long term and short. They have a better overall quality of life.

Diva Tip: I usually spend a lot more for my food than the average person because I buy organic vegan foods at the health food store. I believe that investing in my health will save me money and time. If I am healthy, I am not in the hospital, doctor's office, buying expensive prescription drugs or sick in bed. If I am sick, I lose money when I do not work in some of my occupational endeavors. I save money by not having to buy over-the-counter drugs or visit my doctor 3 to 4 times a year. I have not been to the doctor since I was twelve. I saved a ton of cash when I delivered my babies at home with only my husband as my mid-wife.

4. Car

Everyone needs transportation but not everyone needs a brand new luxury car. It is amazing that a decent car will run you $25k-$30 now. That is a major investment for a depreciating asset. You can buy a house, an appreciating asset, in some states for that amount that can also make you money.

When you purchase a car, you should consider buying it 2 to 4 years old. You will get the car a lot cheaper. You can check The Blue Book to determine the market value before you negotiate. Also, you can even get a report of the history of a car by going to *www.carfax.com*. This will give you an idea if the car is a lemon or had previous accidents which influence the life span of a vehicle. Another way you can get a car cheaper than market value is to purchase it at an auction like I did. You will get it below market value. I got mine $13,000 less the blue book value and I negotiate an additional $1500 dollars off of the car once I spoke with the salesperson. Negotiating on most of your purchases will save you tons of money.

But here is the best way to purchase a car. You let your tenants buy a car for you and you let your business pay for it. How can you do it? It is simple. I wanted to purchase a luxury car at an economic cost. So, I bought a Mercedes Benz 300 that was 4 years old at the end of the year (you get great deals during this time). I got it for $23,000 including taxes etc. and financed it at a low interest rate for $250.00. I bought an investment property that gave me a positive cash flow of $500.00. I invested the first $250.00 into another investment. Next, I took the other $250.00 to buy my car note and put the car in my business name since it was a business car and got the entire tax write off benefits. And I got the benefit of driving a great dependable car at someone else expense. Now that is what I call mastering money instead of money mastering you with high monthly car payments.

5. Entertainment

Divas, who told you that you need money in order to have a good time? Those souls are not thinking and using creative means to have a good time. There are plenty of things that you can do that will generate fun and be more rewarding than going to fun land and riding on the merry-go-round. Here are some fun filled things you can do that are free or cost very little money.

- Book Club Party (with potluck of course) Divas can get together and have a good time discussing a good book that they read and share what it meant to them. Each person can make an inexpensive healthy dish-like a fruit/salad bowl or popcorn. This is a great time to bond with your sister friends inexpensively.

- Have a game night- this is a time when the family can get together to learn how to play new games taught by a designated family member each week. The games could be made up or play the ones we know and love like; hide-in-seek, red light-green light, monkey in the middle etc. You can play card games like Uno and other table games.

- There's plenty of fun out in the sun- you can have a picnic, play outdoor games like football and basketball, go to the play ground or the park to feed the ducks.

- Go to your free public library or community center- At the library, you can borrow books, magazines, videos, CD, and tapes. Your tax paying dollars are coming into use. Also, many libraries put on local puppet, magic and story time shows. When you go to the community centers, they have recreational and educational activities for the kids and their parents.

- Let's get physically fit. I great free thing we can do with our family is to exercise together. Go for a nature walk around your neighborhood. Do yoga on a mat-outside or inside. Go to the park and participate in the free obstacle course. Your tax dollars have already paid for it so enjoy it. Not only will you have fun, you will get physically fit in the process.

Credit Card:
Good Debts vs. Bad Debts

I know you have been taught the old way to believe that any type of debt is bad debt. There is good debt and bad debt. First, let's talk about good credit. Today if you want anything of value, you will need to have good credit. Credit cards help you establish your credit so that you can borrow money for big ticket items like a car or a house. You need a credit card to rent a car and stay at a hotel. In many cases, it's also required for identification purposes and use as collateral for rented items. You should have at least one credit card for emergency purposes. Better yet, it would be wise to have a bank check cashing card that can be used like a credit card. When you make purchases the cash is automatically withdrawn from your checking account. Bank checking cards will keep you out of debt and still give you the privilege of using the card instead of the cash.

DIVA TIPS: I had problems with using budgeted cash money. In my mind, when I had cash on hand, I had free money to spend. Also, I had a challenge with losing money. Psychologically, if I did not have the cash, I did not have the money to spend freely. I used my check cashing card for everything until I got these money issues under control. It helped me not to spend money I didn't have and I stopped losing money. I did pay extra for using my ATM at some places but it helped me solve my problems.

Diva Tip: For credit card repair, check out these e-books, *http:// imdiva.123credit.hop.clickbank.net/* and *http://imdiva.maxfrenzi1.hop.clickbank.net/*

Don't Sweat the Good Debt

Divas, I want you to start thinking a new way that will bring money in your pocket tomorrow by accumulating good debt. Smart, wealthy people have good debt. Good debt is debt that will help you to grow you credit leveraging power and it will increase your income potential.

In the new millennium if you want to financially leverage yourself you must have some form of debt in order to increase your asset potential. Most good debt occurs when you purchase a home, stock or a business. Not many of us have the cash to outright purchase a 100k home or a business and why should we when we can use other people's money to do it. It makes more economical sense, to borrow other people's money to make a purchase instead of using your hard earned money.

Let's me make my point about the power of leveraging by showing you Example A and Example B. In example A, Diva A has $50,000 to invest in real estate. She bought 5 houses worth $100,000 each with only $50,000. On the other hand, example B, Diva B, Ms. Prudent Shopper, has the same $50,000 dollars to invest in real estate. Diva B didn't want to have a large monthly note, so she invested the entire $50,000 in one home worth $100,000. She has a lower monthly mortgage and she will pay off her house a lot faster. She has control of one house that has leveraged her asset to $100,000. Which Diva has her money working for her, instead of her working for her money? If you said Diva A, you are right. Diva B has bought a liability only. The house that she purchased is not making any money for her. She has bought a liability. Though it is a good debt purchase in essence, her investment is not making any money for her now. Yes, she will be able to write off the mortgage interest and she will be building equity. But she is using her income to pay the note for the real estate investment. Even so, the question still remains; did she invest her money effectively and efficiently? Now, let's look at Diva A. She bought five houses. She is living in one house. The other 4 houses she is renting out for $1350.00 per house. After all expenses are paid, she is making a $300.00 positive cash flow from each house. That is a total of $1200.00 of additional income. That income pays the mortgage for the house she is living in. Additionally, she has tax write-off for all houses and her business as a landlord. Moreover, she is now living rent free and her tenants are paying for all of her investments. Now, that is good debt working for you. I love this business.

Really, How Bad is Credit Card Debt

In our country, credit card debt is at an all time high. The average American family has accumulated close to $9,000.00 worth of credit card debt. We all know someone who has more than five credit cards in use. If you have credit card debt from impulse shopping to satisfy your wants- eating out, buying expensive name brand clothes, a vacation trip- you have bad debt. There is no saving strategy here even if you got the item on sale. In the long run, you will pay more for those items than what you bought them for. The credit card company is charging very high interest rate (16% to 29%) for borrowing the money. You are playing double jeopardy and are losing more of your cash if you are paying the minimum payment each month.

Divas, lets own up to the fact that you and I unwisely got in over our heads in credit card debt. And on the other hand, some of us must admit we have lost our minds when we developed the "hobby" of collecting credit cards and charging them up to the hilt. We rationalized that we could afford to make the minimum monthly payments. Credit Card companies did not help the matter by exposing most of us to our first card while in college by bombarding us with slogans that you were a valuable important person if you were a proud card carrier. Unfortunately, you and I did not take the course money management 101. Our ignorance about credit cards contributed to our abuse of them.

Credit card debt is the most expensive debt you can have. This is the first debt you should try to get rid of. I have had credit cards that carried interest rates of 18% to 29.9%. Ouch! To add further insult to injury, this is compound interest. Furthermore, if you only pay the minimum payment, it will take you approximately 30 years to pay it off—and you will pay. Buyers beware. Credit cards companies stay in business by keeping you in debt to them. They make money by charging you interest for using their money. Are they the bad guy? NO! They graciously gave us an opportunity to use the money. They did not force us to spend beyond our means. We did it.

This is the new form of slavery, our bondage to the credit card company. You will have to keep your job just to pay your credit card debt. You can definitely change your circumstances by making it your goal to reduce your bad debt by paying off your credit cards.

Credit Card Debt Deletion

You may want to cut up your credit cards and close the account with the credit card company. This will completely force you to stop using the cards. On the flip side, even if you go through these motions, you can pay them off and start and open up more accounts with new card. You have to make a conscious effort to manage your money well so that if you have a card or not, you will only spend money that you have.

Get into the habit of spending money on your card that you can pay off at the end of the month. If you pay it off within the grace period you will not pay any interest on the money you borrow. Many credit card companies do not like this. They may cancel your card or decrease your limit if they see you are not making them any money. If this happens, move on to the next card. There are many credit card companies out there that want your business.

Diva Tip: Try to shop around for lower interest rates credit cards. There are many on the internet and sent to you via mail. Some have a 0% for the first 6 months and charge no annual fee. A good site that offers information on low interest rate credit cards is *www.bankrate.com.* or check out this credit card site, *http://creditdiva.ecreditdirectory.com*

If you do acquire credit cards with lower interest rates try to transfer your high interest debt to the lower interest rate card. They may charge a transfer fee but your monthly payments will be lower and you can do the Credit Card Debt Fast Payoff Plan.

Another option is if you own a home you can get a home equity loan with a low interest rate to consolidate your debt. Once you consolidate your debt, make a conscious effort to cut up your cards, close your accounts and double up or triple up on your payments. You can even do this method of accelerating payoff even if you cannot get a home equity loan.

DIVA TIP: I contacted my credit card companies with the high interest rates and ask them to decrease my interest. I explained I was trying to pay off my debt and I needed their help. I was a good paying card member and never late, etc. One company representative said she could not do it. I called back the same company and talked to another associate and they did it. Persistence paid off. I called several other credit card companies with the same request. Some did, some did not.

DIVA TIP: If you have a home with equity, you can try to get and equity-line of credit from your friendly banker or credit union. Please e-mail me at elon@thedynamicdiva.com about your creative savvy savings ideas. I'd love to hear about them.

Fast Credit Card Debt Pay-Off Plan

In order to decrease your credit card debt you should have already prepared a spending plan , implemented your savvy saving secrets, and started a savings program with the 3% goal in mind.

If you have done the above, you should have found more discretionary funds available to you. I can imagine another 3%. Continuing from my previous example of Vanessa, the 3% would equal to $75.00 each month you can contribute to paying off your credit card debt.

Let's say you are making payments on your cards on average $500.00 per month. You have 5 cards. First, choose the card with the lowest balance. Card A's minimum payment is $12.00. The balance is $350.00. On your next monthly payment instead of paying just the minimum payment, add the

$75.00 to the $12.00 to total $87.00. This should bring your $350 to $263.00. Do this for the next 3 ½ months and you will have paid off one credit card. Yes!

Now, you take the $87.00 add that to Card B's minimum payment and do the same thing until it is paid off. Do you get the idea? The secret of this method is, by paying off the credit with the lowest balance you will see in a matter of months a card is paid off. This is very motivating. Additionally, you continue to use the cash from the paid off credit card to pay off the next expensive card in-line. This will allow you to pay off each card faster because you will be applying more money from previous card payments to the present one. Follow this technique until all cards are paid off.

DIVA TIP: When I did this method, I felt more empowered as each card was paid off. Moreover, divine intervention stepped in when I got really serious about paying off my debt. Extra money came from unlikely sources. My husband's mom sold her house and gave him $2900.00. We got several thousands back from our income tax return and instead of blowing it on trivial things (clothes etc.), we cleaned up our credit card debt.

Many people have successfully instituted this method and within two to three years they were credit card debt free. Now this method works if you have a car payment or a mortgage also. Some Divas have paid off their house in seven years! Can you imagine keeping one third of your income in your pocket and not having to worry about paying a mortgage for the rest of your life- exciting! By paying off your mortgage, you will have saved tons of money in interest for the loan. Now you have freed up enough cash to invest towards a happy prosperous retirement. Yes, you can do this.

Diva Tip II: Having trouble with your credit card company or want a credit card to do something for you? Check out this website, *http://creditdiva.ecreditdirectory.com*

Great Tax Loopholes

Taxes: Uncle Sam wants your Money

ivas, one of the greatest expenses you will pay over the course of your lifetime will be taxes. If you are employed, have a good government job, **one-third** to **half** of your income will go to Uncle Sam, if you do not create some wonderful legal tax avoidance strategies. The rich Divas understand the importance of legally keeping as much money in your pocket as possible. Besides, the IRS rewards individuals that help keep the economy growing and small business like no other is the fuel that keeps the American economy running.

If you do not have a home based business you need to find one quickly. Unbeknown to you, you are literally giving money away to the government. Full-time employment requires that you give the government close to 40% of your income. If you have a home base business a lot of the cost you would normal spend for various items become tax deductible. Uncle Sam rewards people who have the entrepreneur spirit by allowing legal deductions for the following.

HOMEBASED BUSINESS OFFICE

You can deduct a percentage of your home for the use of your business. This means that if your home is 2000 sq. ft and you use 200 sq. ft of it to run your business from home, you can write off 10% of your mortgage, home insurance, utilities, property taxes, etc.

OFFICE SUPPLIES

Business supplies are legal write offs. Business cards, rolodex, daily planner, pens, pencils, legal paper, glue, are all deductible. You will have to keep the receipts. Please try to keep separate receipts for personal purchase and business purchases. Do not pay for business items with your personal funds. Nor should you purchase personal items with your business card.

FURNITURE

If you buy a computer, fax machine, copier, printer, computer desk, chair, file cabinet, bookshelves etc. to help you run your business like a professional, you will be able to deduct a portion over the course of 7 years or 100 percent all at once. As far as furniture is concern, you can deduct 100 percent or depreciate over 5 year's period. Check with your tax advisor for the facts about your state allowances.

SOFTWARE, NEWSLETTERS, NEWSPAPERS, MAGAZINE SUBSCRIPTIONS AND BOOKS.

If you purchase any type of literature that business related, you can write it off. If you use any software that pertains to your business you may write it off. Computer software is not 100 percent deductible the year you buy it. The I.R.S. believes that most software are good for up to three years, so you have to depreciate the item over a three year period. Purchases of any magazines subscriptions, newsletters, newspapers, books and other periodicals can be written off the year you purchase them.

Business Car deductions

This is a great write off opportunity for those that use their vehicle for business. If you have two cars in the family, you can write off 100 percent deduction for the business car. This mean if you make any repairs, registration, lease payments, parking cost, mileage, tolls, gas cost, repairs and insurance, it's all deductible. If you are buying the car you can deduct the interest rate on the loan and depreciation on the vehicle. If it is a luxury car (you paid $16,000 or more for the car), you can write off a substantial amount.

You get additional breaks with your home office. You can write off 100 percent of business related mileage from your home to a work location and the return trip home. The smart thing to do is to do several business related task within a day and the in between trips can be written off too. To be safe you must keep impeccably records of your travel in a travel log book or your daily planner.

Travel, meals, entertainment and gifts

If your business requires you to travel, you can write off 100% of your hotel, air, railway, rent-a- car, and automobile expenses. Unfortunately, when it comes to eating while on business you can only write of 50% of your meal. If you treat someone to a meal that you may not attend, you can deduct the entire meal. Any other form of entertainment expenses, such as going to shows or playing golf while talking business is 50% deductible. But if you give a gift to a client than it is 100% deductible.

INSURANCE

Self-employed people can deduct 60% of the cost of their health insurance.

Also, if you are a Small business owner or self-employed you can deduct 70% of medical premium for 2006 and in 2007. More important, if your spouse is an employee of the business you can deduct 100% of his/her medical premium and add you and the kids as dependents. What a great relief for you and your family. Please check with your accountant or tax advisor about the particulars regarding this matter.

RETIREMENT CONTRIBUTIONS

If you are self-employed and have SEP-IRA or Keogh, you can write off your contribution on your personal income tax return. Since Bush has been in office he has increased it incrementally over the next couple of years. So, check with your tax advisor about the new numbers for 2007.

SOCIAL SECURITY

The unfortunate thing about being self-employed is that you will have to pay double Social Security taxes. According to the I.R.S., you are considered a both an employer and employee. Hence, you will pay 15.3 percent of your net profit.

TELEPHONE CHARGES

Talk may not be cheap, but at least you can write off 100% of your cell phone bill, telephone and DSL bill if you use all for business purposes. To make record keeping simple, you should have a separate personal line for your family use.

HIRE YOUR KIDS.

Instead of giving your children an allowance, give them a paycheck. It will help you and them in the long run. You can pay kids up to $6,540.00 per year. The tax break is available for sole proprietor or partnership between husband and wife.

CLOTHES

Many people would like to write off clothes. You can write off uniforms legally. You can write off clothes that have the company logo on it as advertisement.

Many of you work two full-time jobs and or part-time job but you may be better off starting a part-time business because the tax saving alone will increase your income by lowering your tax bracket since you can write off a lot of your expenses that once you make this minor income adjustment.

DIVA TIP: Here is one of the best website about tax loophole information, *http://www.taxreductioninstitute.com/group.asp?referer= taxdiva.* Sandy Botkins is an ex-auditor for the I.R.S. He knows almost everything you need to know to legally and ethically avoid paying unnecessary taxes. Get his products if you want to stop giving away or "loaning" your money to Uncle Sam. For more information about Sandy's tax saving products, go to this webpage, *http://www.taxreductioninstitute.com/product. asp?specific=jnnoknh8&referer=taxdiva*

SAVINGS AND RETIREMENT PLAN

Start a savings plan for an emergency fund (no more than 3 months)

An emergency fund is a money market account you create that you put away for dire circumstances that may develop in your life, i.e. you lose your job. These funds should be automatically debited from your checking account into the emergency fund until you get to the desired total. You should put in that account no more that three months of your salary or total budget expense. For example, let's say you salary gross per month is $5,000 dollars. You should plan to have in your emergency fund no less than $15,000 (3 mo. X $5,000.00) dollars.

Start a basic retirement plan (Roth IRA, mutual fund, CD's money market account)

If you do have a 401K or pension plan continue to invest in these plans. But by no means, should you stop there. I have already mentioned that pension plans and 401K plans are becoming extinct with most major companies. They are not fully dependable, nor if you go by those plans will you have enough to retire on. You need to create your own independent retirement plan to supplement these other plans. With that said, try to start a Roth IRA within a DRIPs program. Read the section on DRIPs programs. I like those best because you can do without a stockbroker. Also, Roth IRA stock has a greater growth potential and you are not taxed when you withdraw the funds. Please do your due diligences before you decide on a plan that is best for you.

Invest in Real Estate- homeownership or 1st investment property (3 to 4 homes for wealth builders are a must)

The best way to increase your net worth is to own real estate. I believe to have a true wealth building plan, you need to be invested in several pieces of properties for reason explained in the section on real estate. Just keep in mind, 90% of the wealthy were heavily invested in real estate. It is one of the few investment vehicles that you can get into with no money out of pocket. It is worth the investigation.

DIVA TIP: Ninety percent of millionaires achieved the millionaire status by being heavily invested in real estate. I am interested in real estate investing because it was the investment vehicle that helped me to become a millionaire quickly and achieve financial freedom. Whatever you do, let real estate be your first investment of choice.

ESTATE PLANNING

An "estate" is defined as personal and real property that you own or possess. These items could include bank accounts, real estate, securities accounts, intellectual property or any other asset of value. An estate plan allows you to determine who will manage or distribute your possession in case you become incapacitated or succumb to death. No one likes to deal with life after death matters, but during such times an estate plan would help your family deal with the burden of your financial matters easily upon your passing. The benefits of an estate plan are as follows:

- Professional management of your assets and your care if you are not able to.

- Stop probate- the government taking control of your possession and making financial decisions on your behalf.

- You have the power to determine who get what, when, why and how as far as your personal and real property is concern.

- Minimize estate taxes by passing on your estate to your beneficiaries

You can do your own estate planning or you can hire an attorney to do it for you. At the very least, consult with an attorney about all of your options. Many attorneys have free initial consultations. Here are some of the most popular estate planning vehicles that are available to you.

Living Trust A revocable living trust, also known as a family trust, is for a person or married couple who gives assets to the trust. The person who creates the trust is a trustee. You can operate this trust during your lifetime and after your passing. You can have total control either by you acting as your trustee or by having a co-trustee.

If for any reason you are unable to handle your business affairs. A trustee can take over the management and distribution responsibilities for you or your beneficiary without the need of appointing a guardian of the estate. Appointing a guardian is very costly and time consuming process. In case of death, trust assets are protected from probate and the guardian will make the final determination as to what to do with your possessions according to your instructions.

Will

Creating a Will is a necessary part of estate planning if you want to have a say in what happens to your possessions at the time of your death instead of the courts making that decision for you. You "DO NOT" want to have to go through probate. It can become expensive and time consuming process for all involved. A Will is a simple legal document that will help your heirs identify your assets after all of your liabilities have been settled. You can easily have an attorney help outline exactly how you want your property to be distributed and to whom.

There are many easy Will software packages you can use to create a will. Also, they have adult learning center workshops that take you through the process. But a responsible individual makes financial plans while they are alive and even after their parting.

It is especially important to have a will if you have children. You can appoint a guardian in charge of the assets you will pass down to them and how it should be distributed among your off-spring once they become of legal age. Your children are depending on you to take care of them while you are living and even after your passing. Don't you want to rest in peace knowing that they will be taken care of financially?

Diva

Section II

Investment Vehicles

Diva

Investment Rules

If It Don't Make Dollars, It Don't Make Sense

Y ou should be implementing your wealth conscious tools in your daily routine and developing a conscious capitalist approach to doing business. You are now ready to study and incorporate some of the Dynamic Diva socially responsible investment strategies I have outlined for you. My investment strategies are unconventional and conventional. The unconventional investments are investing in bartering, negotiating, investing in giving and selling-just to name a few. These investments vehicles may not yield you direct capital gains, but they will yield, exponentially, in the quality of life you will have, and the time and money you will save, indirectly, by taking them into account.

All conventional investments such as real estate, businesses and paper asset investing, should yield you a positive return or do not invest in them. Before making an investment decision, you should factor in the following: (1) Inflation, (2) Taxes, (3) Compound Interest, and (4) Return On Investment (ROI). By factoring the aforementioned, you will be able to make a projection on what kind of profit you may incur. Projections do not guarantee you success but do give you a guestimation of your future returns. Make sure they are realistic and not grandiose. To help you fully understand these investment rules. Here is a more in depth explanation of these important investment rules you should take into consideration when you are making your investment decisions.

1. Compound Interest - The Rule of 72

   The rule of 72 shows you the power of compound interest. It gives you an idea of how good a potential investment may be. By using the rule of 72, you can find out how long it will take for your money to double at a given interest rate. All you need to do is divide the interest rate by 72. For example, let's say you have $20,000 invested at 8%, divide 8 into 72. It will take 9 years for the $20,000 to double to $40,000. Now if you took the same $20,000 and invested at 20%, it will take roughly 3 years for the $20,000 to double to $40,000! Here is another example of the power of compound interest: If you had one dollar that double every day for 30 days, how much money would you have in thirty days based on 10%? You would have amassed $40,000!

2. **ROI - Return on Investment**- a performance measure that determines how good an investment maybe. Here is how you can calculate ROI:

$$\text{ROI} = \frac{\text{Annual Profit}}{\text{Avg. Amt. Invested}}$$

For example, let's say you buy a $100,000 house, free and clear, for $100,000 dollars. The house commands a rent for

$1,000.00. The annual income is (12 mos. X $1,000.00) $12,000.00. Your ROI of 12% is not bad. Most investment advisors will say you are doing well if you can get a 10% return on your investment.

$$\text{ROI} = \frac{\$12,000.00}{\$100,000} \text{ X } 100$$

But, let's take that same house for $100,000 and invest $10,000 for the house. Next, borrow the $90,000 from your friendly bank. The monthly payments on the loan is $660.00 and your annual expense is ($660.00 X 12mo.) $7,920. The annual income is $1200.00. Now, minus expenses from the income to get the annual profit ($12,000-$7,920.00 = $4,080.00). The ROI is 40.8%! If you put down 10% on 10 properties and finance 90% of it, you will increase your profit margin more than three times.

$$\text{ROI} = \frac{\$4,080}{\$10,000} \text{ X } 100$$

3. **Inflation Rate**- the increase of goods and service in an economy over a period of time. Put simply, what you pay today for any goods or services will cost more tomorrow. The rate of inflation average is said to be about 3%. So, that being the case, according to the ROI example above, you would definitely beat inflation if you are getting a ROI of 40.8%. It would look like this (40.8% - 3 % = 37%)

4. **Taxes**- When investing do not forget to factor in the taxes. You will have to pay on the gain from your investments. You must know your tax bracket based on your income. It could be 0%,10%,15%,25%,28% or 33% depending on annual income and if you file single or jointly. Get further

understanding of this matter by talking with a CPA or a financial planner.

Before you go a step further, I want to, strongly, reiterate the importance of doing your due diligence before you make any investment. When I invest I take calculate risk. I calculate the numbers and my projection always have a positive cash flow.

Financial Education Investment

Ivas, you must invest in your financial education because if you do not know how to take care of your money there are many people out there who are trained to take care of your money for their gain, i.e. Financial Planner and money scam artist. In a good market or bad market the wealthy *always* make money. Wealth conscious people spend about $500.00 to $1000.00 a year on their financial education and the poor do not because they think it is too expensive. But these same "poor" people would spend $2,000.00 on their credit card, which they cannot afford, for a two week vacation. Go figure.

If you think about it, when you invest $1000.00 dollars that is only $83.00 per month. If you think financial education is expensive try ignorance. It's clear to me and I hope you get it, one of the wealth secrets that wealthy people have honed and you must honed is that they seek to financially educate themselves on a daily basis.

For those of you who are temporarily out of cash, you can go to your local library for free access to many books, CD and

DVD's about money. This is where I got my start. I went to the library and put in a search for books, with the word millionaire in them. I read every book that they had on how to become a millionaire. I read biographies about millionaires. Even today, if I find a book with the word millionaire in it, I will more than likely purchase or borrow it because I want to keep myself abreast of all new information regarding money and you should too. Another inexpensive way to study money is to read the Sunday newspaper business section. You can attend workshops about money matters such as: taxes, real estate investing, debt-elimination and stock investing given by local organizations like the real estate association, SBA or SCORE. Your local adult continuing education centers and community colleges have fantastic cost effective workshops given by local experts that can help you understand your finances and how the economy works. I have used these resources and they have been worth its weight in gold. You can locate these institutions by using the internet or using your yellow pages.

Diva Tip: I spent about $10,000 over the course of a couple of years using credit cards. Even so, that financial education investment netted me one million dollars using other people money. I say that is worth it, wouldn't you?

Diva Tip II: Please visit *www.thedynamicdiva/tools.html* for financial educations tools that will help you reach your goal of becoming a millionaire.

Business Investment

) Buy or Create Businesses – Get Paid Doing What You Love

ivas, owning your own business require more work but if you buy or create the right business you can increase your net worth and leverage your income exponentially. Buying a business is different than buying a job. Most self-employed individuals like a doctors or lawyers buy a job. They have structured their business where they only get paid when they work-linear income. Business owners have a system in place that allows them to get paid if they are there or not. It is called residual income. Another benefit of owning a business is the tax write-off you can take. Most women who are employees cannot write off much and they are force to deal with the glass-ceiling

Hobby to Profit- Create a shoe-string business

Find out what you love to do and figure out how you can get paid to do it. Then create a budget that requires very little start-up money. For example, I love to help people with their financial decisions. I brought into a network marketing business for

$100.00. In my first month in the business I made $1800.00! I got my Securities Licenses for another $1000.00 and made over $100,000. Now the rate of return on my investment (ROI) was over 1000%. Most financial planner will tell you if you make a 10% ROI you are doing good. And it is customary for any start-up business to take 3 years to become profitable. If you have low start-up capital, there is a greater chance of making a profit and increasing your ROI. Here are some businesses that you can start or create on a low to modest budget and on a part-time basis.

Network Marketing

I love the network marketing business! Network marketing is one of the best businesses for women and stay-at-home moms. One thing moms do naturally is to refer other moms to new information that has been worthwhile to them. Have you recently told a friend about a movie, or a sale at one of the department stores? Did this mom take your suggestion to heart and went to see the movie or buy that sale item from the department? Let's say they did. What did the movie theater owner or the department store give you for that referral? You did not get one red cent. Well, network marketing is a word of mouth business that pays you money for referring many people to the product or service you are selling. Another reason why I think network marketing is good for Divas, who aren't afraid to become millionaires, is because most network marketer's success is based on your performance rather than your gender. There is no glass ceiling is this world. Unfortunately, sometimes we still face discrimination in corporate America and government jobs. Also, women are still making 30% less than men doing the same type of job. In network marketing, you are on the same level playing field. Your success and the amount of money you make is based on your performance and following the marketing plan that is set up for you. Here are some other important benefits I like about the network marketing business:

- Low start up cost

- Greater chance of higher ROI

- Learn how to network: networking increase your net worth

- Great motivational seminars and workshop at reasonable rates

- The business system is already setup

Low start-up Cost

Unlike franchises, you can start a network marketing business with an investment of $100.00 to $495.00. The growth potential mirrors that of franchises and other business that require a much larger capital to begin. There are many network marketing companies to choose from. You can find a great network marketing company that suits your interest. Great reputable companies like Aegon, AT&T, Coca- Cola, Avon and Mary Kay are in the network marketing business and have made millionaires out of thousands of Divas. There are network marketing companies that sell financial services, electricity, online store services, legal services, natural herbal supplements and much more.

Greater ROI Opportunity

Most other businesses require thousands and hundred of thousand of dollar to get off the ground. But with a network marketing business you can invest hundreds of dollars with the potential to make the same hundred of thousand of dollars and millions. For example, I invested into a network marketing my initial investment was $100.00 with in three years I had a made over $100,000 in the business. My return of investment was about 1000%. I was in the black in this business the first six month of starting a business. An average business take 3 to 5 years before it is making a profit.

Learn Networking skills

No matter what business you venture into you will have to master network marketing skills. Starting with a network marketing business, you will be taught how to network and build relationships with people. You are giving the opportunity to meet very interesting people of various social economic backgrounds that you can learn and grow from. By increasing your network, you will certainly increase your net worth.

Inexpensive Motivation Seminars

Network marketing companies have the best motivational seminars. In any business you need to stay positive, upbeat and inspired. Network marketing understands this point very well. Network marketing groups provide weekly business meeting, monthly motivational seminars and yearly conventions at a reasonable price. This would cost thousands of dollars if you were to do it on your own. The motivation events are of the same caliber of inspiration as the thousand dollar seminars and in some cases are even better.

Business model is set-up

They have already created a proven successful business model you can copy. You do not have to create a business plan. Book-keeping and accounting tools are available to you and the marketing/ public relation foundation is set in place. This saves you time and money. All you need to do is master the plan, be coach-able, and put the plan to action.

DIVA TIP: In the beginning I thought that network marketing was a joke- not a serious business! Later I came across a friend of mine that did not have the same academic credentials as myself but was making tons of money, spending time with family, and was not working as hard as I was to make ends meet. Like the old adage goes, "if you cannot beat them, join them". I invested in a network marketing business and found it financially rewarding and personally fulfilling. I think this business is great for Divas because we have the unique ability to sell effortlessly. We know how to get women together for meetings, communicate our points well, and help support people on their journey. Also, network marketing is good because for a low start-up cost you can learn about how to run a business, you can do it from home, and you will get great tax write offs. Find a product you are passionate about and willing to buy yourself. Tell a couple of friends about it and watch your business grow. Do not worry about finding a product you like. There are thousands of companies that sale products from health and nutrition, personal care, telephone services and financial services. Do a Google search for the network marketing companies.

Franchise

A franchise is a single business that works within a large chain. The franchiser has an established business model, product or services that the franchisee can buy into. The franchisee for a fee can operate under the popular trade name with the support and training of the franchiser.

The benefits of owning a franchise is that you have access to a successful model and it reduces the trial and error of owning a business. Also, you can start a franchise with little start-up money and strong credit status. Sometimes the franchiser will give the franchisee financial assistance with a down payment.

The challenge to owning a franchise is that you will have to pay a yearly royalty fee, you have limited control of the business and you are not completely your boss because you must follow the franchiser's business guidelines.

Diva Tip: Franchises are decent business but I think in order to make real money you have to own a lot of them. In recent years, the fees and start-up cost have become very high for the most popular ones. It takes over 5 years before you make a profit with some of them. So, be cautious and do your homework before you invest in a franchise. Moreover, consult with a franchise attorney who can give you the low down about the franchise you are looking into. With that said, do a Google search for the low start-up franchises. There are plenty to choose from.

E-BUSINESS

We have left the industrial age and have entered into the information age more than 20 years ago. We have had the great technology boom with the advent of the PC in 1977 and the birth of the internet...... But since the Dot.com bust many people have shied away from the internet as a viable way of making a living. After a five year hiatus, Silicon Valley has awakened and we are on the verge of a new surge in start-up dot.com businesses and now you have an opportunity to get on board as a wonderful new wave of women-owned successful dot.com businesses are being born each and everyday.

The internet is such a great vehicle for Divas because:

1. You can start a web business inexpensively. Today you can purchase a computer for as low as $300.00. The cost for all fees to get your e-commerce web business up and running including internet service provider, web designer, web hosting, shopping cart, merchant accounts have become more affordable. The less money you invest to start your business it will enable you to potentially increase the rate of return on your investment.

2. It can be a home based business. Goodbye brick and mortar stores, hello slippers and home office. Another great benefit to having a web business is that you can start off very small in a room you can create as your home office. You do not need to rent/lease a store front, pay utility bills, hassle with rush hour commute, or deal with employees to successfully run a very profitable business. It is very economical today to start an internet business and millions of people are on the internet looking for great products and valuable information.

   I think the internet is still going through its growing pains as far as being the new way to do business in the world. Divas who honed the skill of generating an income from the internet will be a force to reckon with. The internet is a sleeping giant that is ready to roar.

3. **There is no glass ceiling in the web world**. An internet business would really benefits woman and minorities because in the web world you are judge by your content (information) and not the color of your skin or sex.

4. **A web business is a great source of residual income**. You can get involve with affiliate marketing. This is an opportunity whereby referring people to a product sold on

the internet, and if they buy, you will get a percentage of the sale. To draw traffic to your site and increase sales you can create your own affiliate program on your website. There is Google Adsense. You can post companies ad on your website and when someone who visits your website and click on an ad, you will get paid. They do not have to make a purchase.

5. **Website business is very Diva friendly.**
You can successfully run a business while staying at home with the kids. Matter of fact, you can hire your kids to help you run your business. It will teach them great business skills and can be a tax write off for the business. A win-win situation for you and your family.

INTERNET BUSINESSES YOU CAN EASILY LEARN AND START

Web Designer/Internet Marketing:

A Web designer creates websites for major corporations, non-profit organization, small businesses or an individual. Now it is very easy to design website without having a lot computer and technical experience. There are web authoring software like Dream Weaver and Microsoft FrontPage that have the HTML coding formatted for easy use.

There are online courses on the internet you can take in your spare time for a nominal fee. Also, you can take courses at your local adult learning center or community college.

DIVA TIP: I recommend you read this book about internet marketing: *http://www.quicksales.com/app/aftrack.asp?afid=542180&u =www.internetmarketingsweetie.com*

Electronic Marketer or Search Engine Optimizer:

This is an up and coming industry of professionals who are employed or act as consultant with major corporations and small businesses on how to increase traffic to their website for greater sells conversion and public relations initiatives. The goal is to increase page ranking on internet search engines and directories like Google and MSN. The high page ranking may lead to more traffic which in turn may increase more sells of the company's products.

This is a highly recommending skill for website owners, web designers and web developers. The income from this industry for good electronic marketer and SEO specialist can range from a few thousands to hundred of thousands depending on how they incorporate this profession in their business plan.

E-commerce Web Business

You can sell products or services on the internet. You can have a large store but contract your entire inventory to other manufactures and they will drop ship the products. What this basically means is that you will not have to have any inventory in your house, mail out any product nor have the hassle of having employees.

It is a whole lot easier doing financial transactions over the internet today. E-commerce sites have greater protection from credit card and identity theft. Shopping carts software has improved buying transactions.

HERE ARE SOME OF THE MOST RECENT WAYS YOU CAN MAKE MONEY ON THE INTERNET:

1. Affiliate Marketing

Divas, you do not have to own a computer to do affiliate marketing. Affiliate marketing was popularized by Amazon.com. Amazon.com gives a commission to anyone that recommends an individual to Amazon.com to a purchase a product. You are given a link that you can put on your website, flyer, business card etc. When someone uses your link to access products from Amazon. com, Amazon.com gives you a percentage of the purchase price. It is just that simple. Make a referral and get paid for it. Like Amazon.com, there are many companies that give such an opportunity. All you have to do is go on the internet, key in **affiliate programs: product of interest (affiliate programs: books)** and search to your hearts content. I have an affiliate program that you can join for free too! Just go to *www.thedynamicdiva. com/affiliate* and earn from 25-50% commission on many of the products I sell on my site. I'd love to share the profits!

DIVA TIP: For a very good affiliate marketing ebook, *http://im-diva.quitdayjob.hop.clickbank.net/*. Another affiliate marketing e-book I recommend is, *http://www.quicksales.com/app/aftrack. asp?afid=542180&u=www.affiliatemarketingsweetie.com*

2. Sell products you make

Create hard (tangible products) products like Books, CD, DVD, Newsletters, Magazines that you can sell online. Also, you can create soft products (intangible products) like e-books, teleseminars, podcast, webinars, and online courses. These are very inexpensive products you can make since the bulk of the product is information.

3. Teleseminars–

Teleseminars are an inexpensive way for you to hold a seminar via the telephone in the comfort of your home-in your PJ's if you like. Thousands of Divas are giving up the commute, renting of a facility, and other cost involved with putting on a seminar. You can save a lot of time and money without giving up the great revenue obtained from doing a Teleseminar. It is a win-win situation for both parties.

The expert gets to do a full-fledged teleseminar (30-500 listener on the line) from her home. Let's say after she cooks dinner for the family, she goes to her home office and talks an hour or two on her topic. She e-markets the class and her shopping cart takes care of all the payment transactions. Her clients can download the seminar online from her website. After the teleseminar, she can return back to her favorite night activity, a nice warm bath and in bed at a responsible hour. She can sleep soundly knowing she is making money in a couple of hours that use to take weeks for her to make. She is learning to work smarter with her time and her money.

The recipient of the teleseminar, from the comfort of their home, will get great important information that will improve their lives. They save time and money from a commute, getting dressed in expensive clothes and spending more time away from the family. This is the life!

4. Webinars

Webinars are like teleseminars, but instead of using a phone, you use the website like an online TV to do the seminar. This is becoming very popular. Unfortunately, it does require one to know specific computer skills in order to put it all together. It is very do-able. I like them because many people have different learning styles. For those that learn better visually and in a classroom style setting, webinars are the best choice.

5. Online study courses

This is a course that a person can pay for and take online in the privacy of their home at a time that is convenient for them.

Let's say you have offered a course teaching tax loopholes for a small business. You write up the online course with a quiz and final test. Sell it for $10-$15 per click. This is another example of residual income. You can make a product one time and sell it at anytime to thousands of people all over the web. The profit potential is limitless!

6. Internet radio show, i.e. Pod casting

You can do an internet radio show online with very inexpensive and minor equipment. On the show you can promote your products and services, interview great people and sell advertisement space on your talk radio site and provide commercial advertisement while doing the show.. The show will instantly establish you as a media expert and give you great access to reputable guest on your niche talk show topic.

7. Selling advertisement on your website

You can make money by selling advertisement on your website. A good source to immediately start having businesses advertise on your website is to sign-up for Google Adsense. Google offers businesses the opportunity to advertise on Google for a fee and any other website that the content matches the keywords of the business. This give the business a lot of exposure all over the world wide web and they do not have to pay for it until someone click on their Google ad. This benefits you because each time the ad is clicked on your site you get paid. To find out more information on how to monetize your website quickly with ads go to *www.google.com/adsense*.

Another thing you can do to get businesses to advertise on your site is to post a banner or *advertise here* link on your site. A lot of small start up businesses charge $50.00 per month for a business to advertise on the site. The more popular your website is and the higher it is ranked on Google, MSN and Yahoo it may increase other businesses buying ad space. For this reason it is very important to invest in learning Search Engine Optimization (SEO). With SEO, you learn optimization techniques that may increase your website page ranking in search engine like Google, the God of the search engines, or MSN. This will lead to millions of people looking at your website daily that search your keywords. The more visitors you have daily of a particular market group, the many companies that advertise to that market group will want to align themselves with you.

8. Do online surveys

Yes, believe it or not there are many people making decent living doing survey on the internet. A survey is a form you fill out giving your honest opinion about a product or service. There are online chats for group, focus group and product survey that you can participate in. Depending on the survey you can get paid $1 to $75 for an average survey. Some will pay upwards of $150. The time spent filling out a survey can range from 5 to 60 minutes. That is time well spent if you can make $50 for filling out a survey for one hour.

DIVA TIP:You can find cash incentive surveys at *www.signup.greenfieldonline.com* and *www.surveysavvy.com*. Here are more incentive survey sites for your perusal: *http://imdiva.surveysc.hop.clickbank.net* and *http://imdiva.paidetc.hop.clickbank.net/*

9. E-books–

E-books are electronic books that people can download from the internet. They are very simple to produce and very cost effective. The main thing you need to make an e-book is Microsoft Word to type the book. Next, Transfer the book to format it in Acrobat Adobe PDF. Post the e-book to the internet for a fee. It is truly that simple. You save so much money. The best e-books to sell are information or how –to-e-books.

DIVA TIP: I recommend this great e-book about information products that you can make and sell for a profit on the internet: *http:// www.quicksales.com/app/aftrack.asp?afid=542180&u=www.informationproductsweetie.com*

BUSINESS PLAN

Divas, I know you are excited and ready to go, but before you start a business, it is wise to have a business plan. A business plan is a map that outlines what your goals are and the techniques you intend to use in order to make your business work. You will be able to answer such questions as: who will be my clientele, how will I market to these individuals, what will be my expense, and how much money to I intend to make? The serious Divas know that a well-thought out plan, even though time intensive, will increase the chances of success tenfold. Most Diva's businesses fail because they didn't have a business plan.

If you want to get financing or upstart money from banks and other financial institution, you will need to have a very professionally business plan. Banks want to know before they loan you the money, what actions you have taken to ensure your success and minimize some inherent risk involved with owning a business. Even though, I highly recommend that you try to start your business with your own money, you should give the same attention that a bank would to see if you should invest in yourself. All of the businesses that I am recommending to you have very low start-up cost that range between $500-$2000 dollars. It not about the money, as much as it is about the time and commitment you will sacrifice that will give this business a chance of survival and the ability to thrive.

A well designed business plan should be written especially for you. Use your creative energy, imagination and visualize the type of business you want to bring into existence. Do your research. Talk to other business owners. There are free and very low fee community organizations that can help you prepare your business plan.

A business plan will give life to your ideas. It will help you to put a plan of action in place to make your dream of running a formidable small business a reality. You can make this business plan simple or elaborate.. When you complete the plan, type it and post it where you can see it daily. Keep another copy in your files. Your business plan will change overtime. Don't be afraid to revise it. Have fun!

Visit *www.thedynamicdiva.com* web site for your free Business Plan Outline.

DIVA TIP: Now that your business plan is completed you need to take the following simple steps to run a legitimate small business:

1. Get a small business license

2. Open up a business checking account

3. File a federal tax I.D. with the internal revenue service.

4. Get a sales permit

5. Join the local SBA, SBDC or contact Score

6. Set up an office in a room of your home

7. Form a Business structure, Sole Proprietor, LLC, SCC Corporation

You have now completed all of the step that will have you up and running. And you are in full compliance with the I.R.S. as a legitimate business for tax write-off purposes.

DIVA TIP: I would not leave you without a business plan guide resource book. Here it is: *http://imdiva.businesspl.hop.clickbank. net/.* You should look at this one, too: *http://imdiva.ezybizplan. hop. clickbank.net/*

Real Estate Investment

Real Estate Investment

Real Estate - House Rich

ivas, we all know that one of the basic necessities in life is shelter. Everyone needs a place to call home. This is why investing in real estate is a sure bet. Real estate is the best way to break into the wealth building process. Matter of fact, I recommend that each person have at least 3 rental properties plus their home as part of their wealth building plan. Here are some of the pros to owning investment property:

- You can get started with no or little money out of pocket

- It is a great hinge on inflation

- Great legal tax write-off

- Excellent form of collateral for borrowing money with no questions asked

- Instantly you can increase your network and leverage power

- You can buy with good credit or bad credit

- Create positive cash flow- additional income in your pocket monthly

- Income properties are a form of residual income-you must have residual income investment vehicles as part of your wealth building strategy!

No Money Down Deals are Real-Info-mercial work!

No money down means that cash does not come directly out of your pocket to purchase a piece of real estate. You can take equity out of your home for a down payment and closing cost for a purchase. You can borrow one hundred percent of the value of the property and have the seller pay the closing cost. You can have the seller carry back 20% of the value of the home and get first financing from a lender. Even better, you can find a foreclosure property or distressed properties. These are the best deals because you can make an arrangement with the seller to takeover payment for the house and give them money to get back on their feet. In return, you may get a house for less than 10k out of pocket! Your credit does not have to be checked and you may have bought it below market value.

Real Estate can hinge inflation

The average appreciation rate each year for a home is 6 % per year. The average rate of inflation is 3% to 4%. This is very important for investment sake. Whatever you invest into has to either beat inflation or rise comparatively. The value of real estate will usually increase because the products to build a house will go up along with the value of land. Additionally, what you charge for rent will increase over a certain period of time. Remember, people need a place to live-one of the basic necessities of life.

Real Estate tax benefits

When you buy real estate you have many legal tax loopholes. As an investor you may be able to write off property taxes and repairs done on the property. As a landlord, you can use one room in your home as your office which may allow you to write off a percentage of your utilities bills, your mortgage and car expenses. Contact a CPA for further understanding of tax benefits.

Borrow money from your house

The good thing about a house is that it is a form of collateral. Banks are willing to give you equity line of credit against your house because if you do not pay they can easily take your house away. With that in mind, loans are easy to get in case of an emergency. I call it the "life happens" moments, i.e. you need a bond for a family member, you need money to send your kids to college or you need money for medical bills. Or you can begin to build wealth by investing into another piece of real estate or purchase a business.

Real estate can increase you net worth

Your net worth is determined by subtracting your liabilities from your assets. This will give you the value of what you are worth financially. Real estate tends to grow on average 5% each year so if you were to buy a house for $100,000 within a year the value would increase by $5000.00 ($100,000 X 5= $5000.00). The value of the home goes up on a yearly basis because the cost of the material and the land continues to rise yearly.

You can buy real estate with good or bad credit

Real estate is a stable risk for the lender, they are willing to be flexible with the terms to loan you money to purchase it. If you have great credit you will pay less for the house. Conversely, if you have poor credit, you will pay a lot more for the house. Paying more for a home is not a bad thing, if the value of the home appreciates significantly and increases your net worth dramatically. The worse case scenario is that you can refinance the home for a lower interest rate as you improve your credit rating.

Additionally, if the loan-to-value in a house you are buying is less than 75%, the lender may be friendlier with the terms because it is of a lesser risk for the lender.

DIVA TIP: Sub-prime loans are not bad if they can get you into a home with a sub-par credit rating. Sub-prime loans are a problem if you cannot afford to make the payments. Most of the real estate I purchased was with sub-prime loans, but I made sure that I could make the payments on my owner-occupied R.E.., and I could charge enough rent to cover the cost of the mortgage payments on my investment real estate. If you cannot afford the mortgage payment, do not purchase the property. It is that simple.

Create Positive Cash Flow

Positive Cash flow is money left over after all expenses are paid on a rental property. Let's say you purchase a home for $100,000. The mortgage and escrow (taxes and insurance) are $800.00 per month. Additional expenses of $200.00 bring your total expenses for the property to $1000.00. You charge your tenant rent at $1350.00 per month. The income from your tenant minus the expenses gives you a positive cash flow of $350.00 per month and $4,200 per year. If you do ten of these deals, you will have positive cash flow of $3,500.00 per month and $42,000 per year of positive cash! Moreover, because it is not income, you may not have to pay taxes on the money. Check with your CPA for greater understand of this matter. You have now replaced your income or added more revenue to your bottom line.

Some of the real estate investment techniques that you should study and implement are as follows:

- Fixer-Uppers- rehab and sell: buy low and sell high deals

- Buy and hold- creates positive cash flow deals that should appreciate-go up in value-over time.

- Foreclosures/distress properties- Buy low and sell high deals

- Tax Lien sales- buying real estate pennies on the dollar

- Speculative R. E. Buy - gamble on the hope the R.E. will appreciate.

DIVA TIP: Here are some low cost e-books that will educate you about about the following real estate investment options:

Tax liens: *http://imdiva.taxliens1.hop.clickbank.net/*

All types of R.E.: *http://imdiva.refortunes.hop.clickbank.net/*

Foreclosures: *http://imdiva.guyburger.hop.clickbank.net/*

Various R.E.: *http://imdiva.cash4homes.hop.clickbank.net/*

Using your IRA to invest in R.E: *http://imdiva.iraebooks.hop. clickbank.net/*

How to Finance Your Real Estate Dreams

Financing is a very important part of investing in real estate. You may not have to use your money to buy real estate, but you do have to choose the right lender to finance the real estate for you. Keep in mind, these institutions are working for you and you need to find a lender that is a right fit for you and your real estate investment goals. You can usually find a large selection of these financial institutions by looking on the internet, newspapers, yellow pages.

Here are some institutions you can research to finance R.E. loans:

- Commercial Banks
- Saving and loans
- Credit Unions
- Mortgage Brokers
- Mortgage Bankers
- Private lenders
- Pension funds
- Life Insurance Companies
- Government Loans (FHA/HUD/VA)
- Owner financing

DIVA TIP: Personally, I have successfully used mortgage brokers. As an investor your package has to be set up properly by an investor mortgage broker that knows what lenders like to see on a 1003 Uniform Loan Application. The mortgage broker is more incline to educate you about how to put such a package together for the lending institution. A mortgage brokers can shop your loan package around to many lenders. I do pay more with a mortgage broker but I get information and education that is worth its weight in gold.

DIVA TIP: Read this e-book that will share with you the truth about the mortgage industry and give you the best advice on how you can get a good mortgage with good or bad credit history: *http://imdiva.mortgage11.hop.clickbank.net/*

Here are the types of loans some of these financial institutions offer that may meet your R.E. purchasing needs. They have loans for everybody but be very careful. Borrowing guidelines have become so flexible that people are now qualifying for loans that they may have difficulty paying back. If you have difficulty choosing a lender, contact me via email at *elon@thedynamicdiva.com* and I'll try to help!

- Low Down payment loans
- One hundred percent financing loans
- Bad credit loans
- No-income verification loans
- Debt-consolidation loans
- Fixed and adjustable rate loans
- 125% refinancing loans
- No Doc (no income, no asset verified) loans
- Bankruptcy loans/foreclosure pending loans
- 40 and 50 year mortgage loans (New)
- No down payment loans

DIVA TIP: Be very careful when choosing a loan because you, and not the lender, will be responsible for making those payments. I have been in the mortgage business and I have seen a lot of people taken advantage. Many got into loans they could not afford. On the other hand, I have seen many Divas advised not to purchase a home because it was out of their price range and they still went to another lender who approved the loan for them.

Nina

Stock Investing

Wall Street Wonder Woman

iva, investing in the Stock market is a smart way to prepare for retirement and with the benefit of compound interest, get a good return on investment based on the dollars you invest. There are some very basic techniques that many books discuss on investing in the stock market such as buying mutual funds, stocks, treasury bills, bonds, and index funds, money market accounts and CD just to name a few. I recommend you look for books that focus on those types of safe investment vehicles that gives you average returns. This book focuses on some wall street investing that I think Divas should pursue that will generate a greater return on their money than the 6% to 8% you can get from a basic investment guidance.

Diva, you will be required to get an education regarding most of them but I think it worth the high risk higher return opportunity. Do not be intimidated by investing in the stock market. Stock investing is legal gambling but the risk does not have to be high if you educate yourself about the stock, use your female intuition and your common sense when making your investing decisions. One rule of investing is to invest in things you like and use often. Another thing to consider when investing in stock is to invest in products that people cannot do without like, food, clothing and shelter. One thing is clear and studies have been done that show that novice investors fair pretty well against choices that stockbroker and expert money gurus have made.

I believe that if you keep your emotions at bay and your greed in check, you can be a very successful knowledgeable trader. The most encourage aspect of trading today is that you can do it anytime of day with access to a computer. Also, you do not have to put a lot of time or days into trading once you understand the system of each trading discipline. This is ideal for women who want to stay at home and make money in their pajamas. Imagine, Divas, taking a couple hours a day to make an extra 2 to 3k month.

Divas should look into Drips, Hedge funds, Stock Options, Currency trading, Futures and Commodity Trading.

Do not be intimidated by your lack of knowledge regarding them. There are plenty of resources and courses you can take to develop a greater understanding and win the game of investing on Wall Street. Here is a brief definition of investment vehicles you should be investigating.

DRIPs Plan:

DRIPs stand for Dividend Reinvestment Plans. Many companies allow individuals the opportunity to buy stock directly from the company via a transfer agent in very small amounts on a monthly basis. The reason it is call dividend reinvesting plan is because you can reinvest your dividend or capital gains without the assistance of a stock broker. Even better, many companies do not charge a fee for reinvesting and you can increase your ability to buy more shares using this approach. The benefit of having a DRIPs is that you can invest a small amount in safe blue chip stocks like Walmart, Home Depot and AT&T and have complete control of your accounts. In essence, you become your own stock broker. There are over 1,000 direct investment plans to chose from and they have a plethora of good information on the internet to help you chose the best drip stock for you. Since the invention of the personal computer and the internet DRIPs investing is just a click away. Here are some transfer agent site were you can easily purchase DRIPs stock: *www.equiserve.com*, *www.melloninvestor.com.*,*www.bankofny.com* , *www.investpower.com*, and *www.wellsfargo.com*. You can do international DRIPs investing also. You can get direct-purchase ADR contract by way of *www.adr.com* and *www.bankof ny.com*.

Hedge Funds:

Hedge funds are usually entertained by the wealthy and institutions. Hedge fund can perform a lot of creative strategies like selling short, leveraging and program trading since they are exempt from many of the rules and regulation that control mutual funds. The funds cannot have more than 100 investors and the average investment can range from $250,000 to 1 million dollars. You may not be able in the beginning stages of your investment journey to participate in hedge funded plans. However, you can work on other investment vehicles that will generate the income to invest in this type of funds in the future.

DIVA TIP: Do you want to invest in a hedge fund created by The Dynamic Diva and quicken your rise to becoming a millionaire? Well, I may have the investment vehicle for you. If you are interested in finding out more information about investing in hedge funds, serious wealth builders can email me at Hedgefund@thedynamicdiva.com.

Stock Options:

A stock option is a contract that gives an investor the right to buy (call) or sell (put) a fixed number of shares-about 100-of a given stock at a given price for a specified period of time. The stocks could be commodities or indexes. The purchaser hopes that the stock's price will go up, if he bought a call, or down, if you bought a put, at a price that will provide a profit once he or she sells the option.

The best part about purchasing an option is that you can put a small amount of money down to control large amount of stocks. In turn, investing in stock options increase your chance of acquiring a higher return on your investment and you can make a profit in a shorter amount of time in comparison to investing and buying stocks out right. This gives you an opportunity to leverage your shares of stocks.

You do need to extensively educate yourself about stock option trading. But it is well worth it. It is not as risky to do stock option trading once you have a very good educational foundation. Besides, a lot of software packages and online trading companies allow you to do mock trades to help you become comfortable with stock option trading. Once you are successful at mock trading, then you are ready to do the real thing. You can set up an account online through one of the online trading companies.

Currency Trading:

The Foreign Exchange Market (forex) is the largest market in the world. It is estimated that close to $2 trillion dollars worth of currency is exchanged daily. Currency trading is very hot now. One of the reasons for its popularity is that the U.S. dollar's value has declined significantly and a lot of financial gurus feel it is not worth very much today because it is not back by silver any longer. Additionally, U.S. stock market returns have been very bearish (low) over the last 5 years that many people are looking at other financial markets to invest into to get a greater return on their money. Divas, you should too.

Currency trading is a form of day trading that involves exchanges between one currency for another currency. For example, the popular trading has been the exchange of U.S. dollars for Euros. The currency is traded in pairs and the trader buys the currency she thinks will appreciate and generate a profit. The most popular exchanges have been the US dollar against the Japanese's yen, the British's pound and the Euro.

Forex trading educational material is vast. You will not have a problem finding out information and education on the internet. You can read books but the internet usually has the most up-to-date information but you do have to weed through the scams in order to get to the legitimate ones.

Commodity Trading:

Commodity trading is the trading of raw materials such as corn, wheat, silver, gold , oil and soybeans. Commodity trading is based on a supply and demand where investors buy and sell commodities via futures contracts. When trading commodities, you want to remember to buy when prices are rising and sell when prices are falling.

There are a lot of books and a plethora of information about commodity trading on the internet. You can do a Google search on the subject but be careful of the scam information. For further understanding of this subject and stock options read this great book ABC's to Commodity Trading by S. Clark. This book is concise and to the point. It doesn't have a lot of fluff. It is written for the beginner investor and for the seasoned investor. It has quizzes to help you familiarize yourself with the subject and chart your progress, plus she offers a free consultation if you refer a client. Ms. Clark, personally, and successfully invest in commodity and stock option trading making an awesome profit and she is willing to show you how you can make full-time money on a part-time basis trading.

DIVA TIP: You can get a great book about commodity trading at *www.abccommoditytradinghandbook.com*

Futures trading:

Futures trading involves trading at an auction market in which individual and companies buy and sell commodity/futures contracts at a specified date in the future. Future trading is performed in a trading pit were stockbrokers openly yell and hand signal their bids.

You can invest in futures with no or very little money out of pocket. It is the same concept as investing in real estate. You have possession of a high valued commodity with out paying for it outright. This is a good leverage investment vehicle. Here are some future products: wheat, oil, Eurodollar deposits, gold, foreign exchange, the S&P 500 stock index, etc.

Once again, like most of the other investment vehicles I previously mention, most the literature will tell you that these are very high risk investments that should only be entertained by seasoned or expert investors. Season investors were once beginning investors who studied the market, did mock training and invested safely by using discretionary funds in the beginning to learn and earn. They practice and acquired the educational know-how to help them graduate to the point where they are making a comfortable living. Divas, these are all skills you and I can acquire. Moreover, I know that by taking the time to learn about these types of investments it will help to diversity our investment portfolio and improve our chances of getting a greater return on our money, rather than going the traditional route and competing for the oversaturated low return mutual funds and stocks that are in the market now.

REITs:

Real Estate Investment Trusts (REITs) are developed when a corporation or trust gathers a group of investor's money together in one pot to purchase and manage income property. REITs are traded on major exchanges just like stocks. They are also granted special tax considerations. REITs are very attractive for Divas who want to invest in R.E. without the responsibility of owning real estate. Unlike owning investment property, REITs are very liquid, and you can own a variety of R.E. like hotels, malls and commercial property. Another reason why a lot of Divas prefer to buy REITs over actually owning properties is that REITs pay yields in the form of dividends no matter how the share performs. That simply means you can make money in a bad or good real estate market.

There are many REITs who participate in DRIPs. Read the section on DRIPs to fully understand the benefit of this investment approach. DRIPs allow you to invest in the stock market by buying them directly from the company without a broker and have the dividends reinvested without a fee. This will increase the level of shares you can acquire and dividend check you will receive.

DIVA TIP: Here are some great e-books on various trading opportunities:

Forex: *http://imdiva.1forex.hop.clickbank.net/*, *http://imdiva.fx profits.hop.clickbank.net/*

Here is a great e-book/video on how to do Stock Options, Forex and Currency trading: *http://imdiva.fibmaster.hop.click bank.net/*

Bartering Investment

Bartering Investment

Barter: Bargain Trade Secrets

The reason why many people do not barter is because they do not want people to think they are cheap. They feel it is unprofessional. They are afraid people will reject the bartering and that they will not get a fair exchange for their services or products. Oh contraire, my Diva friend.

Bartering is an agreement between parties to exchange goods and services without using money. We do it all of the time but many of us have not utilized it to its fullest potential. Many do not seriously consider it a viable investment tool. I beg to differ on several accounts. You are missing out on a fun way to save money and increase you investment pool.

I learned the importance of these techniques years ago from a bankruptcy attorney before I began my wealth journey. He would barter his attorney fees for cars, vacation trips, remodeling work on his home, just about anything. He had clients he helped that had skills. One of the main ways to make money is the ability to limit the spending of money while simultaneously allocating more money into your investment pool. If you are using cash to pay for everything you want and need it decreases the amount of money you can use toward vehicles that will make more money for you. Remember you want your money working for you instead of you working for your money. What better way to do this than by bartering your way to riches.

Here's a great example of bartering. I am considering hiring a live-in nanny to take care of my two boys while I run my home based business. In exchange for free room and board valued at $750.00 per month. She will take care of my boys for 30 hours out of the week doing light cooking, cleaning and teach them how to speak Spanish. I will pay her cash $500.00 per month. Now let's break down the saving potential here.

To have a nanny come to my house to watch two boys ....$1,600.00 per mo.

Both boys taking Spanish lessons.............. $500.00 per mo.

Cooking & cleaning .... $500.00 per mo.

Total..**$2,600.00 per mo.**

I would save $1100.00 per month. Wow! What a great deal for both. She would get a great home to live-in with weekends off. My kids would learn a skill that would help them make new friends and who knows maybe they will use their bilingual talents in a field of interest. Or, maybe they will choose to visit poor Spanish speaking community to help empower them to reach their dreams too. And more important, now it frees up time for me to write the books and monitor my online wealth building website, *www.thedynamicdiva.com* so that you and I can make more money doing the things we want to do!

Diva, bartering is very wave nouveau. The celebrities do it all the time. They are the product. Celebrities barter their fame everyday for clothes, jewelry, trips, hotel accommodations and much more. My favorite Diva, Billionaire, Oprah Winfrey, uses this technique very well and in a big way. You may have seen her show were she will discuss her favorite things and shares them with her audience. She gifts her audience members with slippers, coffee, jam, bras, make-up, you name it. The audience is excited and appreciative for the many gifts given to them by Oprah. But did Oprah go to the store and pay retail price for all of those lovely gifts to surprise the audience. That would be very expensive. NO!

The owners of these great gifts barter with Oprah to give the items to the audience in exchange for the invaluable and inexpensive publicity. Oprah is viewed by millions of people all over the world. She has the Midas touch and influence over all of her loyal fans to buy what she likes. By the mere mention of the companies name people flock to the store to buy the products because they want to be like Oprah and partake of what she does. They may not be rich and famous like Oprah, but they can eat and drink the same coffee and wear the same slippers and bra. What a great deal for the company. They get a tax write off since the gifts are considered promotional items and great free press. While Oprah gets the opportunity to play Ms. Clause and give her audience a wonderful reason to think she is great and puts a smile on their face. It is a win-win situation for all involved. Do you think this maybe one of the reasons why she a billionaire? That is with a **BIG B**. This is an example of bartering at its very best. What can you barter?

Nina

Negotiating Investment

Negotiate Everything

You maybe are wondering why I consider negotiating as part of my investment vehicles. I have found that on my wealth journey that negotiating the price for various items have save me thousands of dollars that in turn have made me hundreds of thousands of dollars. I took the saved cash and invested into various investment vehicles that have given wonderful return on my dollars. One thing I have learned to do is value every penny and made sure it is working for me at all times. Giving unnecessary money away foils my plans of economic freedom. Everything has a price but that doesn't mean you or I have to pay for it. If you want to leverage you funds you must make negotiating apart of your investment repertoire.

Divas, let's set the record straight from the onset, **EVERYTHING IS NEGOTIABLE!** Why pay the retail price for something when you do not have to. I pride myself in always trying not to pay retail for most things that I buy especially big ticket items like a house or a car.

What authority said you have to pay the retail price for anything? I have found from personal experience that most people are willing to negotiate. Also, negotiating works best in some venues and does not work best in others. But in all venues, you have the right to negotiate. Here are five sure-fire, easy Dynamic Diva negotiating techniques that can save you hundreds of dollars!

1. **The number one key to successful negotiating is in the asking.**

   There is a saying that is true to heart, a closed mouth does not get fed. In other words, if you do not ask, you have already lost or missed out on a great deal. In the game of negotiating, 90% percent of successful negotiating is in the asking. Ask the seller if he is willing to negotiate his price. Or better yet, you can be the aggressor in the matter and start the negotiating.

2. **Start the negotiating.**

   By you starting the negotiating process, you have caught the seller off guard. He is usually not prepared to negotiate because most buyers that he deals with do not ask for a lower price. Service providers or sellers do not negotiate very well when they do not anticipate a negotiator. Hence, you are at a slight advantage because the seller is forced to think on his/her feet and most people do not negotiate well when they are unprepared to negotiate. With that in mind, they are more willing to be more conciliatory during this time and give you a great deal just to get the sale.

3. **You must ask nicely:**

   You would think that this is obvious, but it is not. I have experienced and witness many individuals be very rude, defensive, caustic and demanding while trying to negotiate. They go into the negotiating combatively. Negotiating without the right approach will definitely kill the deal. Like the old adage states, you get more in life with honey than you do with vinegar.

When you ask for a deal, please use a non-threaten voice and do not be aggressive with your approach. For example, I recently had to get a tree cut down at my home. I always get three estimates for everything I get done, you should too. Especially, if you are inexperienced about the subject and unfamiliar with the going rate. The first tree cutter charged $350.00 for the job. The second tree cutter gave me an estimate for $375. And the third tree cutter stated $750.00. I explained up front that I am getting several estimates and I am looking for good workmanship and economical, **not the lowest bid.** When each tree cutter gave me their price, I state calmly, **"I was hoping for a lower price. Can you do better?"** Stop now and practice that statement. (I will wait) Most often, they will pause, think and give you a lower price. Some people will stick to their guns and not waiver. That is their choice and you have the choice to not do business with that person also.

4. Lastly, ask (humbly) one more time. Say in the gentlest voice, **"Is that the best you can do?"** If they state yes, then thank them for their time and let them know you will think about it and get back to them if you are interested. If they give you an even lower price you can go for it or thank them for their time and get back to them later. This works for me like a charm. I always get the best price by asking twice.

Back to my example of the tree cutters and how the five Dynamic Diva negotiating techniques worked for me. The first cutter's price of $350.00 would not budge. The second cutter's price of $375 went down the first time I asked to $350.00. Then the second time I asked him, he went down to $325.00. Later, he called and stated that he would do it for $280.00. The third cutter would not budge on the first or second attempt. But, he called the next day and offered to do the job for $700.00. He was disappointed when I told him that we already gave the job to someone else.

Who do you think I chose? You are right, the one that was willing to negotiate. He wanted the job and he got it! Imagine if I had taken the $750.00 dollar estimate without asking. I would have lost the opportunity to save/invest $470.00($750-$280.00 = $470.00)! That is a lot of money I kept in my pocket by just asking two simple but important questions: **I was hoping for a lower price, can you do better? And, is that the best you can do?**

5. **Make it a win, win situation for both parties to benefit from the negotiation**: Be reasonable when you negotiate. And keep in mind, the seller desires when you negotiate. Usually, the seller main desire is to get a sale that will bring them a profit on the deal. For example, the tree cutter I finally decided on was already working in the neighborhood and I promised him I was going to give him more business. I had another tree on a nearby rental property I needed to have cut down. He was going to get repeat business and he did not have to travel far to do the work which saved him gas money and time.

Give negotiating a try; I am sure it will work for you too. Practice will make you a better negotiator. Treat negotiating like a game on items you do not care about to perfect your negotiating skills before you do the deals that mean a lot to you. What did I do with the money I saved? I took the $470.00 and invested it in my son's stock investment vehicles. Yes, I am not only saving money but I am making money with the savings now. You can too.

Nina

Dynamic Diva Dream Team Investment

iva, you should invest the time and energy to organizing a group of expert in various fields to help facilitate your wealth building. It is essential that you have a business attorney, mortgage broker, wealth mentor, insurance broker, banker, and a CPA on your team.

An attorney will help you with the legal ramification of all of your business goals. They can handle a lot of your contractual agreements. You are in business now and you will want to be very professional about all of your business transactions. This being the case, all of your business transactions should be in writing. Verbal agreements only, do not carry much weight in the court of law. We live in a very litigious society and you may have your share of court dates.

Another important Diva Dream Team player is a Certified Public Accountant (CPA) The CPA will help you organize your books, keep your records straight, educate you on tax loop holes, file your tax returns and keep you in Uncle Sam's good graces.

A mortgage broker will be able to connect you with a large pool of lenders to help you purchase real estate according to your R.E. goals. It is easy to find the property, but it is more challenging to find the right lender to do the deal. You will need the aid of a good investment R. E. Broker to find the gem properties that fit your R.E. investment initiatives.

The insurance broker should be able to take care of the many kinds of insurances you will need to put in place to help you protect your wealth. Now, you do not have to work with one agent to purchase all of these insurances. You should get agents that specialize in some of these insurances. Here's a list of insurances you will need to acquire.

- car insurance
- health insurance (self-employed Diva need this),
- business insurance
- property insurance
- disability insurance

Bankers are, usually, your ticket to low interest money. Even though banks are known for having very strict guidelines and not very flexible, you should become friends with your neighborhood banker. Lately, because of the increase in competition for your money, banks are becoming more flexible and lenient with their lending process. By developing a good rapport with your local banker, you will build the necessary trust and relationship to acquire personal and business loans or equity-lines of credit. Banks love to loan money to business owners that bank with them, and they know and trust.

Lastly, you should seek the assistance of a wealth mentor; they can probably connect with your dream team because they have their network of wealth builders. Wealth mentors are wealthy people who have probably tackled most of the challenges and success involved with becoming financially free. They can easily lead you on the right path and support you on the journey. For more on this subject read the section on mentor investment.

When you are searching for your Dynamic Diva Dream team, keep in mind, you can find some economical advisors. Most real estate broker, insurance broker, mortgage broker and financial advisor do not charge a fee but make money from a percentage of the product they sell you. You can find a reasonably priced bookkeeper that can help you with your books and they have great advice as far as your taxes are concern. It is not always true that the more you pay for professional advice, the better it is. But I will admit, I am assured quality information and education from top quality advisors because they have the prestigious connections and are involved with the best deals that average folks to do not have access too.

DIVA TIP: I like to connect with people that specialize in my field of interest. I have an intellectual property attorney, real estate attorney, and I have an options coach and many wealth mentors. I have a prayer partner that helps me stay spiritually aligned. I have a mate that is very supportive and a part of the Dynamic Dream Team. It is so important for you to have a love one on your side. It makes the wealth journey so much more attainable.

Nina

Intellectual Property Investment

Get Paid for Your Ideas

Did you know you can get paid for your knowledge and ideas? Your ideas are intangible asset that are defined as intellectual property. A lot of Divas are making a lot of money by legally protecting their ideas by acquiring patents, copyrights, trademarks and licensing for their products or services. Why is protecting your intellectual property so important?

One reason for legally protecting your knowledge is so that they are not stolen and used by others to make money. For artistic and personal reason, you do not want someone to take your name or product and use it for negative purposes that shine an uncomplimentary light on you. Lastly, and most importantly, you can take your intellectual property and license it for a profit. Licensing is a billion dollar industry. Many Divas make a lot of money by licensing their ideas to various companies and individuals. Licensing your product or services benefits a Diva because it is a formidable way to leverage you and create residual income. Let me show you how it has work for some famous companies and keep in mind it can someday work for you too.

You see, by licensing your product or service, you keep the rights and control it, but give someone or some entity the permission to sell it and profit from it. In return you will receive compensation in the form of royalties. In essence, each time they sell an item you will get a percentage of the profit. Moreover, by licensing your product or service, you do not have the risk involve with manufacturing, the licensee takes on that responsibility. This means you do not have any:

- Employees

- Sales cost

- Inventory

- Risk

- Investment-no money out of pocket to profit from this endeavor

This is a great form of leverage because you create another form of revenue stream without any work on your part beyond getting your information legally protected.

Bill Gates, the riches man in the world, used this licensing to propel him to billionaire status. This software program I am using now to write this book was licensed to the computer companies to put in their machines and he sells the upgrades to me to continue using the product. Think about the billions of people today that are using his software programs!

Licensing is great for the small business because you may not have the financial resources to build your business nor do you have the desire to build a company like Bill Gates. I know of an inventor who creates things with the sole purpose of licensing because he can make millions of dollars without the large amount of time, energy, risk and financial resource involved with creating a big company. This is a prime example of working smarter instead of harder.

Let's look at and understand a little about each of the other well known intellectual property ideas.

Patents

A patent is an exclusive right granted by the government to a company or person for an invention. The exclusivity right last for a period of about 14 years. This basically means that no one can take your idea and profit from it without your consent. If they illegally, market your invention and profit from it, they will can be sued and may have to pay some form of restitution.

For example, Robert Kiyosaki shared a tragic story about his experience with not acquiring a patent for his Velcro wallet. The patent was $10,000. He thought it was too expensive so he went on to create and sell his Velcro wallet. They sold like hotcakes. You may have had one yourself. Other enterprises companies saw the popularity of the wallets, copied and sold them too. After a while, because Robert was too cheap to invest in a patent, the market became saturated with a lot of copycats and drove him out of business.

On the other hand, if he had a patent he could have done two things: (1)Have a complete monopoly over the product for 14 to 20 years, (2) Even better, he could have licensed the rights to all of the other companies and acquire royalties from each and everyone of the copycat companies. The best mistakes to learn from are other people mistake. I hope now you understand the importance of protecting your ideas with a patent.

DIVA TIP: To find out more information about how to acquire a patent or to patent your idea, with the U.S. Patent and Trademark Office, go online to *www.uspto.gov.* The importance of consulting with a patent attorney to make sure it is filled out properly must be factored in as well,

Copyrights

A copyright is the exclusive right to create and sell copies of literary, musical, artistic, software and electronic and other written materials. Some examples of copyright materials are books, songs, websites and software.

DIVA TIP: To find out more information about how to copyright your work, go to *www.loc.gov/copyright/*

Trademarks

A trademark is a unique name, symbol, motto, or design that legally identifies a company or its products and services, and it prohibits private or public parties from using identical or similar marks.

For all legitimate businesses branding has become very important because it give a business its identity. Years ago, it was mostly practice by small to large companies, but now that businesses can grow quickly a lot of home-based start-up business are getting in the act of branding themselves from the onset. If a business is to be recognized as a legitimate business it must have its own name, logo and motto. For example, when I created my e-business *www.thedynamicdiva.com*, I trademarked the website, logo and motto. I came up with a unique name women can easily remember. A logo that reflects the name and a motto that would peak interest and set me apart from other women owned online businesses.

DIVA TIP: To find out more information on how you can acquire a trademark go online to *www.uspto.gov.*

Software

Software is new to the industry but follow the same rules as the others. You can create a contract that will protect the application, rights and registration of software. Most software packages are licensed. A software license allows a person or company to legally purchase and install a software program on a computer or network

DIVA TIP: It is safe to say that you should hire a intellectual property attorney to handle all of your contractual procedure. You can do your own copyrighting, patent and trademark applications online, but I highly recommend, you get legal advice if you want to do the process correctly. It is a very complicated subject that only knowledgeable professional attorneys possess. Do your homework because they are many attorneys who will work for a reasonable fee. You will have to search them out.

Nina

Networking Investment

etworking increases net worth: It takes a rich village to raise lots of dollars.

If you want to increase your net worth, invest the time and energy in improving your networking skills. The more people you come in contact with and share information, resources and love, the greater chance you will inspire them to want to be in your presence and partake of your ideas, inventions and information. Wealthy people do business with people that they know and like. Take the altruistic approach. How can I help you accomplish you dream?

The best strategy for your networking is for you to focus on how you can help the other party accomplish his/her goals. Be genuinely interested in helping someone out. Get a persons business card and e-mail address when you meet with them. During the conversation, find out what are their dreams. What brings them joy? People love to talk about themselves. Be a great listener and find something of interest that you can assist them with. Keep in contact via e-mail periodically; send a note or follow-up with a phone call. Be genuine with your efforts. By helping others fulfill their dreams or solve a problem, in return they may be able to help you do the same. Sometimes it may not come directly from that person, but they may introduce you to others who may benefit from your product or service.

Mentor Investment

I t takes a village to raise a millionaire. And in the village, there is a Diva or Divine man, who can help you accomplish your endeavor. A mentor is an essential piece of the wealth building puzzle that can give you the information, education, network and inspiration to help you reach your goal. No matter what investment or wealth dream you may want to fulfill, most often, someone has already done it before you. More important, they were successful at accomplishing the feat by making all of the necessary mistakes and enormous financial lost.

What an advantage you have working with a mentor. He or she will save you time, money and decrease the pitfalls involve with becoming wealthy. In a nutshell, they have been there and done that. They have a proven, sure-fire formula or technique that they have used to get where you are trying to go. If you want to be a millionaire, you need to associate with them, read their books, go to their seminars and workshop. Heck, if you are really smart and bold, ask them out to lunch or coffee to get their advice on your investment dreams. You may be pleasantly surprise at how giving they are. Millionaire mentors are truly happy people and they love to share information. Like most people, they love to talk about themselves and are proud to share their accomplishments. They will give you priceless information (gold nuggets) that can catapult you to riches.

Let me be the first to tell you that you cannot achieve wealth on your own. I did not get to this level of financial security by myself. I am truly not a self-made millionaire in essence. I could not have accomplished my goal of becoming a millionaire if it were not for the people who have guided, nurtured and supported me on this wealth journey. Even today, I have many mentors who assist me.

One thing I want to make clear Diva is that you can find a mentor via many sources. A lot of wealth gurus take advantage of the mentorship deal by giving you the impression you have to spend a lot of money and go to 3-10k seminars to get the wealth secrets. Seminars are very good and beneficial. I give them and I participate in them. But, I do not advocate that they are the only way or even the best way to accomplish your wealth dream. These events do not guarantee you success, but they do increase your chances since you have direct access to the mentor that knows how to manifest wealth.

Even with that said, when you think of a mentor, you are limiting yourself by thinking that it comes directly from a person. You do not have to invest a lot of money to become wealthy. Many of you, Divas, may be financially challenged. But remember when I started my wealth journey; I was temporarily out of cash too! I did not have the immediate funds to go to expensive workshops but I did have a library card to get books to motivate me and read real estate information to help me make money. Matter of fact, it was via real estate books, tapes, CD's and inexpensive adult learning centers that I learned and used R. E. techniques that made me hundreds of thousands of dollars. One book in particular that stands out is, Robert Allen's, *Multiple Streams of Income*. I used one idea in the book, which was less than a paragraph, to net me 30k on one deal!

Divas, I found my greatest mentor via the spirit inside of me. I trust that the spirit within was enough courage, faith and inspiration that I needed to help me accomplish my dreams. With God as your mentor, what can you not accomplish?

Nina

Selling Investment

Sell, Sell, Sell: Sell service or product, and not your soul

Get comfortable with selling. Sellers are the ones who get to wealth a lot quicker and faster. More important, do not put that energy out in the universe, that you cannot sell. You are selling yourself everyday to make friends, a date, buy groceries, get a discount on a dress you saw at Macy's and get the loan to buy a house. Some may be very subtle forms of selling but never the less a sell is a sell. If you learn these few techniques I will share with you, you will become a good seller and on your way to millions. Remember, people who sell are the ones that get to wealth a lot quicker and wealthy people are sellers. Let's look at some notable ones: Oprah, Jesus, Mother Theresa, Angelina Jolie, Tyra Banks just to name a few.

Diva Tip: It not about the sell as much as it is about the people who love to buy—focus your energy on the buyer. I do not sell to people. I serve people. As mentioned earlier, I focus on fulfilling a need or a dream.

People buy from Divas they like and can relate to.
If you have a likeable personality people will naturally gravitate towards and be interested in what you have to share. People trust people that they like and they want to help them. What better way to help a friend than to buy her product or service.

People buy from Divas who are genuinely passionate about the service or product.
People buy into your exuberance about the product. They have to believe that you believe in the product. If they sense you are trying to make a quota to pay this months bills, you have lost them and the sell. Have a sincere love for what you are doing and selling and you will attract many buyers.

People buy from Divas who are knowledgeable about service or product.
Be the expert that you customer is looking for. We are in the information age. People are willing to pay top dollar for information on a subject. They want the best and most up-to-date facts or information. You have to stay on top of your product and service and be available to provide them with it on demand. They want to be in the know so you must be a know-it-all about your product or service. This will set you a part from the rest.

People buy from Divas that are happy, funny and have a great disposition.
If people feel that you enjoy what you do, they will want to be apart of the fun. People have to deal with so much negativity and life and they do not want it to be a part of their purchase process. So have fun with your product/service. Serve up a joke or two and put a smile on your client face. It will go a long way.

People buy products or seek services that will solve their problem.

They are looking for you to solve their problem and quickly, please. Get to the point of showing them how your information or product will save or make them money; help them find more time to do the things they love; help them lose weight and make them feel healthier and less tired. If you can get to the heart of someone's problem and your product is the panacea, then you won't have any problem selling it. Don't be afraid to sell.

Nina

Giving Investment

I **Invest in Giving**

nvesting in giving is a key factor in guaranteeing that you will continue to receive according to the natural laws of the universe. Giving is a natural progression to an abundant lifestyle and wealthy people adhere to giving gracefully. They can afford to do it. I do believe in tithing at your place of worship and giving a portion of your earnings to various charities and organizations.

But, I do not believe in giving money to charities when you cannot afford it. It is very counterproductive. I think it is very unwise and not economically smart to tithe when you do not have the financial resources to take care of your basic necessities for living. I have witnessed many people tithe and increase the wealth of the church and pastor while they are still living in poor conditions trying to make ends meet. These same people cannot pay their electrical bill or send their children to a decent college nor have a retirement plan in place for their golden years. They give begrudgingly and out of obligation because they fear that the wrath of God will be upon them if you are giving out of fear and not from the heart, you blessing will be blocked.

Divas, charity begins at home. You are your first sacred temple and you are honoring God when you take care of you before you take care of anyone else. I recommend Divas you take a more responsible approach to investing in Giving. This approach will not only benefit you but it will benefit your favorite charitable organization in the long run, also.

Here is how investing in giving works. You must first accomplish the Dynamic Diva Pre-Wealth Plan before you start to tithe or give to any charity organizations. This means you have to get your finances in order: have a sound spending plan; pay off your debts; prepare a retirement plan for yourself; and have a college or business fund set up for your kids. During this time, you can still give to your place of worship or charitable organization by volunteering your time, donating meals and becoming financial secure.

By becoming financially secure, you will free up cash that was once devoted to paying off debt and impulsive spending. Also, you will create the financial resources to genuinely be able to afford to give ten percent or more because your investments will yield a ten plus return that will enable you to give back.

Doesn't it make since for you to work on increasing your income so that you can increase your tithing? For example, one client refinanced her house and was able to pull out over $300,000. She gave $30,000 to her church and invested the remaining funds into a R. E. that would generate a monthly income of $3500.00 and increase her net worth. This was enough money for her to live off of for the remainder of her life.

Keep in mind, you can legally write off $11,000 dollars if you give to a family member. Also, most of the tithing you give to churches and charitable organization can be written off also. Uncle Sam rewards you for being a giver. For further understanding of charitable tax deductions, contact your CPA or the I.R.S.

If this proves to be too difficult to stop contributing to charities for a period of time, then I would minimize my giving to 3% of my monthly income until you have completed the Dynamic Diva Pre-Wealth Building Plan. Once that plan is successfully completed, I am sure you will create the necessary fund to give merrily and substantially.

DIVA TIP: I am a believer in the famous quote, God helps those who help themselves. And in turn, by taking care of your business, you will be rewarded with the necessary funds to care for others.

I, personally, do my tithing unconventionally. I believe that charity begins at home so I tithe to my immediate and extended family. Giving comes in so many ways, not just financially. You can give your time, your attention, information and your prayers. Most of all the gift of giving is love.

Nina

Diva

SECTION III

Diva Millionaire Myth

Diva Millionaire Myth

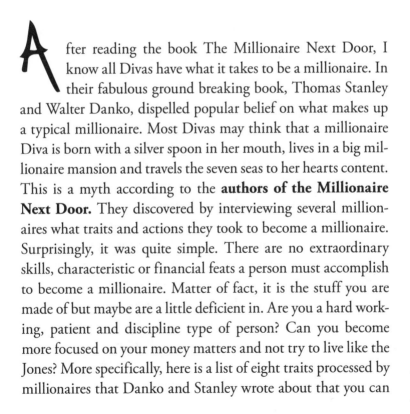

After reading the book The Millionaire Next Door, I know all Divas have what it takes to be a millionaire. In their fabulous ground breaking book, Thomas Stanley and Walter Danko, dispelled popular belief on what makes up a typical millionaire. Most Divas may think that a millionaire Diva is born with a silver spoon in her mouth, lives in a big millionaire mansion and travels the seven seas to her hearts content. This is a myth according to the **authors of the Millionaire Next Door.** They discovered by interviewing several millionaires what traits and actions they took to become a millionaire. Surprisingly, it was quite simple. There are no extraordinary skills, characteristic or financial feats a person must accomplish to become a millionaire. Matter of fact, it is the stuff you are made of but maybe are a little deficient in. Are you a hard working, patient and discipline type of person? Can you become more focused on your money matters and not try to live like the Jones? More specifically, here is a list of eight traits processed by millionaires that Danko and Stanley wrote about that you can acquire with a little discipline and practice. The millionaires next door were people who accomplished the following:

- are self-made Millionaires
- lived below their means
- married and stayed married.
- lived in a modest home in a typical middle class neighborhood
- drove older cars
- penny pinchers/cheap folks
- invested time, money and energy on financial education.
- saved and invested for the long term

I hope I have taken the mystery out of becoming a millionaire and I hope you are excited and can now see why I believe you can do it. You can easily make adjustment to your lifestyle and take action to emulate the wealthy. The good news is that you process within you all the skills and qualifications to become wealthy now. And if you do not have it, you can learn it.

Even with that said, the way prices for houses, cars and a college education are rising, you need to be a millionaire just to make ends meet-slight exaggeration. But, what hit home to me, is the fact that a million dollars today is not a lot of money. You certainly cannot retire on it. I consider it a good financial start and I want you to also. I think it is important that you set very high standards and expectations for your financial goals so that you cannot only attain them but do well with the money you make. Money is not there for our own self-aggrandizement but to serve the community and the world.

DIVA WEALTH TIP: Do not misunderstand this important fact, with the rate of inflation, a million dollars does not have the value it use to have. Millionaires are just getting by. One cannot retire on such meager earnings. But it is a wonderful start to catapult you towards the multimillionaire status and maybe we all can graduate and be like Oprah when we grow up-a billionaire. But not just any billionaire, but one who invests their money to make difference in the world.

Diva

Conscious Capitalist and Socially Responsible Diva Millionaire

iva, one formidable aspect of developing a wealth consciousness is that you want to create the financial means to make money that makes a difference in the world you live in. Capitalism has such a negative stigma attach to it that it turns many people off. Ones first thoughts about a capitalist are individuals who are amoral, greedy opportunist that exploit people, destroy the land and the environment to make money for themselves and their few little friends. One of the main reasons why so many people are disinterested in making money is because no one wants to be a part of a society that uses it for ill means. I, personally, struggled with this for many years because I was thinking I would rather be poor than make money that would continue the vicious cycle of *greed*. I only saw the bad money was doing in the world and not the good. This is one of the main reasons I chose poverty and maybe why you have too. I asked myself how I, with a good conscious, can join a society that uses money for all the wrong reasons. Eureka! I found the answer in Conscious Capitalism. I, consciously, spend, save, invest and give my money to banks, investment companies, businesses, charity organizations and people that their mission is to do productive, positive things with money.

A conscious capitalist strives to intermarry the morals, values and ethics with every transaction that they make with their money. Spirit is back in the workplace. As a conscious capitalist, you strive to earn money from your good work and spend your money with people and businesses that do well in their community, society and throughout the world.

When you make the decision to invest you want to do Socially Responsible Investing (SRI). As a socially responsible investor you want to put your money where your mouth is. Invest in companies that speak your truth, maximize your financial returns while contributing to the social good. You want to align yourself with companies that:

- Promote environmental protection and safety

- Honor diversity in the workplace and humane conditions

- Produce quality and safe products that will not harm but promote wellness

More specifically, SRI allows you to invest in companies that promote affordable housing, education, living wage jobs for all people, universal healthcare and factors in environmental and ecologically sound practices when they're making all of their business decisions because they know it impacts the world. Socially responsible investors stay away from companies that produce pollution, guns, tobacco, sweatshops, pornography and exploit individuals for the sake of capital gains.

There are many businesses, mine included, that cater to a holistic approach to doing business. The goal is to put people first. The philosophy is to serve the public by using our economic power responsibly in order to create a better world today and for future generations to come. As a conscious capitalist, I can go to bed with a clear conscious knowing that everyday my money caters to helping empower people and create a sustainable environment so that we can live in love, peace and harmony. Simply put, my money is doing good work in the community, nation and world.

Nina

Dynamic Diva Wealth Builder Plan

Now that you realize you have within you all the skills it takes to become a millionaire Diva, here is an outline that will get you started in accomplishing your goal. Our first objective is to replace your income with positive cash flow investments that will provide you with monthly income that will take care of your monthly expenses. By replacing your income, you will be financially free. This semi-retirement status will allow you to focus your energies on fulfilling your God-given talents or maintaining your new found retirement status.

Now let's see how this could look for you. I am going to give you two scenarios, Dynamic Diva Wealth Builder Plan I (**DDWBP I**) and Dynamic Diva Wealth Builder Plan II (**DDWBPII**). **DDWBPI** is for those Divas who want to get there quickly, and I hope that is for all of you because wealth waits for no one. The second scenario, **DDWB II**, is for those Divas who wants to take the tortoise approach-slow but steady. The benefit of this plan is that you can start it on a part-time basis.

Dynamic Diva Wealth Builder Plan I (DDWBP I)

1. Complete the Dynamic Diva Pre-wealth Plan

2. Create residual income-purchase 10 Single family homes at $100,000 per home. Each home, after all expenses are paid (mortgage, taxes, insurance, etc.) will generate a positive cash flow of $300.00 per month. This will give you a monthly positive cash flow of $3000.00.You will be the owner of one million dollars of real estate! If you did your due diligence in selecting the property well, each year the real estate will appreciate at least 3% and build your net worth.

3. Develop an internet e-commerce business that will bring you in revenue from sponsors, affiliate marketing, and sell from your information and drop-ship products. A well search engine optimized site and pay per click should easily bring you more than enough traffic and sales to generate $2000.000 per month net profit once all of your expenses are paid.

4. Stick to your spending plan and combined both incomes from your small business and your real estate to net you $5000.00 per month. Your CPA will help with keeping your books sound and may be able to help you keep the majority of the $60,000.00 in your pocket with sweet R.E. and small business tax write-off. Please check with your tax advisor about this matter.

5. Now that you are financially free and no longer are stressed over your money matter, you can take all of your time, money and energy to exercise your life purpose. You should continue building your R.E. portfolio and your internet

business to combat inflation. Take some of the additional money beyond the $5000.000 dollar and invest in some of the suggestions given in the wealth building plan investment guide. Keep in mind you want to invest in vehicles that will give you 20% return on your investment (ROI).

It truly is that simple-not easy-but simple. By following step 1, 2, 3, you are on your way to becoming a Millionaire Dynamic Diva!

Now for the Divas that are interested in taking the Tortoise approach, the DDWB II plan is for you.

Dynamic Diva Wealth Builder Plan II

1. Complete the Dynamic Diva Pre-wealth Plan

2. Create residual income-have an owner-occupied home and purchase 3 investment properties worth $50,000 to $100,000. Each property should generate a positive cash flow of no less $300.00 per month after all expenses are paid. (Tenant pays you a rent of $1100.00- your expenses $800.00 = $300.00 profit). This will give you a positive cash flow of $1500.00

3. Keep your day job and start a part-time home-based small business in a field you already have experience in. This allows you to start your business easily because you do not have to learn the skill. The income from the business after one year should generate $1000.00 per month. Once again, check with your CPA for small business owner tax avoidance advice.

4. This will give you a combined extra income of $2500.00 from your home-based business and R.E. investment properties.

Dynamic Diva Wealth Building Prototype, "Penny Sense"

"Penny Sense" is an actual outline of a Dynamic Diva Dollars Wealth Building plan I put together to help Divas become financial astute, reach financial freedom and graduate to the millionaire status. To protect the identity of the individual I have changed her name and altered some of the financial information. This outline will not guarantee success but it will give you an idea for how you can put together your own plan. Or you can copy hers with some modification that will fit your financial goals and your present financial situation.

This plan was created for educational purposes only and does not guarantee these financial projections for anyone. All investments come with inherent risk and for legal protection I will advice you to seek professional counsel regarding all of your financial, tax and legal matters.

"Penny Sense" Brief Bio:

Penny is a 35 year old African-American, married woman with three children ,ages 8, 11 and 13. She is a self-employed hairstylist. She owns a home. She is in charge of her finances. The combined income of her family averages $5,000.00 per month or $60,000 a year. She has great credit. Her average FICO score is 730. She wants to become financially free.

FIRST ASSIGNMENT

She filled out the Wealth Conscious Quiz, 3D's Financial Statement, 3D's Income and Expense Report, Dynamic Diva Dollars Agreement Contract, and her short, intermediate and long term Dynamic Diva Dream financial plan. Let's look at each plan in detail.

Wealth Conscious Quiz
3D's Financial Statement
3D's Income and Expense Report

Wealth Conscious Quiz

She scored 50% on this quiz.

Upon talking with her, she unconsciously kept telling me "you cannot do that" every time I mentioned a money idea. She was very afraid of money and had a poverty consciousness regarding money.

Diva suggestion: Penny had to practice the wealth conscious skills: prayer, meditation, affirmation (Wealth Chants), visualization and journaling for 21 days.

DIVA TIP: You can take the same quiz at *www.thedynamicdiva. com/Dynamicdivamillionairequiz.htlm*

3D's Financial Dream Plan

1. Short term Goals (1 year)

    - She wanted to pay off all of her bad debt (credit card and car payment).

    - Buy her first piece of rental property.

    - Start a home-base business.

2. Intermediate Goals (3-5yr.)

    - Pay for her son's college education and semi-retire from her job.

    - Build enough residual income so her monthly expenses are paid.

    - Have at least 10 pieces of rental property and online internet business generating $5000.00 per month.

- Fast forward her retirement plan because she had very little in saving in her mutual funds.

- Have medical insurance, disability insurance for herself and her husband.

- Have college funds available for her other 2 children.

- Have a will.

3. Long Term Goals (10 years)

- To be retired.

- To become a multi-millionaire so she can live her life purpose.

- She was unsure of her purpose but she is seeking within to find it.

3D's Financial Statement
Assets

Penny's Financial Statement:

Cash (liquid asset)- Checking Account	$800.00
Cash (Liquid Asset)-Savings Account	$200.00
Securities-stocks, mutual funds	$4,500.00
Life Insurance (cash surrender value)	$0
Personal property (autos, jewelry, furniture etc.)	$30,000.00
Retirement Plan (IRA, 401K)	$ 0
Real Estate (market value)	$120,000
Total Assets	**$150,500.00**

Liabilities

Current Debt (credit cards, accounts)	$9,000.00
Real estate mortgages (house)	$62,000.00
Personal Property (autos, jewelry, furniture, etc)	$10,000.00
Total Liabilities	**$81,000**
Net worth (Assets-Liabilities)	**$69,500.00**

3D's Income and Expense Report

Income (Penny and Husband)	$5,000.00
Additional Income	$0
Expenses	
Mortgage Payment (Impound Acct.)	
Property taxes	
Homeowners Insurance	
HOA	$950.00
Household Expenses	$350.00
(Utilities, water, phone, cable)	
Car Payment	$600.00
Gas	$120.00
Food (eating in & out)	$400.00
Entertainment	$300.00
Clothes, personal items	$300.00
Miscellaneous	$200.00
Credit Card payment	$500.00
Retirement plan (mutual fund)	$150.00
Total expenses	**$3870.00**
Total Income-Total Expense=Discretionary funds	
($5000.00-$3870.00	**$1,130.00**

SECOND ASSIGNMENT

Need vs. Wants list

Penny looked at her income and expense report. She needs to determine which items on the list she could eliminate to increase her discretionary income. She did her needs vs. wants list. She wants to use the left over money after her bills are paid to pay off her bad debt and invest in real estate and e-commerce business.

Upon completions of her Needs vs. Wants, She created an additional income of **$500.00** per month by decreasing her clothing purchases, basic cable plan, basic cell phone plan, eliminated eating out and minimized her entertainment expenses.

Dynamic Diva Dollars Income Replacement Plan or Semi-retirement Plan

She decided to buy investment property that would bring in $3000.00 of positive cash flow. Her online web-business would generate $2000.00 per month of income from her beauty supply drop-ship & affiliate marketing. The $5000.00 generated from these two residual income businesses would replace her and her husband's income.

Dynamic Diva Credit Card Fast Payoff Plan.

Penny's credit card debt was $9000.00. Her and her husband's combined car loans came to $10,000.00. She decided to refinance her house and take out $20,000 to payoff the debt. The new loan she got decreases her monthly mortgage expense by $23.00. Her monthly mortgage went down and not up. Also, her monthly expenses decreased by $1,100.00 dollars per month with the elimination of her car notes and credit card debt. So now she put **$1,123.00** back in her pocket.

Savvy Saving Secrets Guide

She invested in bartering: One of her clients is a graphic designer/web developer and they worked out a deal for her to exchange services. For car service, one of her clients is a mechanic who repairs her car in exchange for hair care. No money out of pocket deals.

She invested in negotiating: Saved $400.00 on a new air system for her home. She brought new tires and save $100.00 by asking for a discount.

She invested in saving: Shops online for discount coupons on food. She has her children help her do surveys online for additional income. She increases the insurance deductible for her car and home to $1000.00 and put an additional $100.00 in her pocket.

New Dynamic Diva Spending Plan (aka Budget)
She did her new spending plan. She decreased her monthly total monthly expenses by $1,723.00. WOW! So her new spending plan increases her discretionary funds to $2,853.00 per month. Now keep in mind, all she did was organize her finances, decrease her wants and got rid of some bad debt. She did not change jobs nor get a raise. Actually, by reorganizing where she allocated her money, she gave herself a raise.

Dynamic Diva Dollars Auto-Pilot Payment Plan:
Penny decides to do her banking online and set up an automatic deposit and bill payment plan with her bank. This would save her time and money. This action also took off the pressure for her to stay committed to her new spending plan. All she needed to do was to have her employer deposit her check into her account. Her bank would pay all of her bills. Also, she has

her DRIPs investment company plan and emergency saving plan automatically debited from her checking account to help her stay committed to her new savings and investment plan. She put her discretionary funds of $2,853.00 into these accounts. She is on her way to financial freedom.

THIRD ASSIGNMENT
CHOOSE A WEALTH BUILDER PLAN
(DDWBPI OR DDWBPII)

Penny Sense's Dynamic Diva Dollar Millionaire Wealth Builder Plan

Penny has chosen to do the **DDWBPI**. She wants to get to the semi-retire level fast.

She decides to start accomplishing her first goal of building wealth by investing in real estate. More specifically, she has chosen to do 100% rehab/permanency loans for 10 single family homes. Each house she purchased for $60,000. She did minor rehab and increase the value to $115,000.00 per home. With cost of rehab about $12,000 per house, her final loan amount was $76,000. She has 34% equity in each of the properties. She rented the houses for $1,000.00 per month. Her expenses for each house were $707.00. She has a positive cash flow of $2,970.00 per month. Remember she got these properties with out any money coming out of her pocket and she increased her cash flow. Lastly, she has accumulated, including her primary residence, eleven pieces of real estate with a total value of (11X $115,000) $1,265,000! She increased her net worth by $385,000 giving her a grand total of $455,000 close to ½ million dollars in one year.

Next, she started her first home-based e-commerce business

because the start-up cost was low and the rate of return on her investment would be higher. She had great credit, no bad debt and a good financial statement. She got a small SBA loan for $25,000 to start the business. If things go well her potential for return within 18 month is $100,000. Her rate of return is 25%. This is the number we like to hear. It will only take her 4.2 months to make back her initial investment. She should pay off the bank loan in one year. She used other people money to start her R.E. investment and small business investment dreams. There is no money coming out of her financial resources to start these investment ventures. She invested in good debt to leverage her income potential.

Since she was starting an e-commerce web-business at home while still maintaining her full-time job, I suggested she do a business she had experience in or love to do as a hobby. Upon extensive brainstorming, she decided to do something online regarding hair since she is a hairstylist with a cosmetology license to teach. Her goal was to educate, inform and serve her clients with important information about hair care and sell hair care products, self-publish hair care booklet, do-it-yourself online Webinars, Teleseminars courses. She would make money selling her products that would be drop-shipped to her clients. She would not have to stock inventory nor do the shipping herself. She would make money selling advertising and sponsorship to business who wanted to reach her clients via the internet. Since her off-day from work was Monday she would have her Teleseminars on Monday. This is a phone conversation she would have with several people on one line.

Here is how a Teleseminar works. Let's say, you have a Teleseminar on starting your own hair care business or how to do your own hair permanent like a professional. There are 20 people on the call paying $19.95 for one hour. That would make her $399.99 for one hour of work. If she has 4 Teleseminars per month, that should bring in an average of $1200.00. This is just one portion of revenue she can draw from her internet site. She would go to a vendor fair in hair care to set up the drop shipment process or join an affiliate program with a hair care online internet company. When her clients would link to them from her site, she would get 15%-20% on each purchase that they make. She could generate another $1000.00 from the drop-ship business and if she sales ad space she can make an additional $500.00. This would give her a total after 18 months of $2700.00 per month. This would give her a grand total from both investment vehicles $2970.00 (R.E.) +$2700.00 (e-business) = $5670.00. She made it to financial freedom!

I have yet to mention the tax loopholes she creates with both businesses. To protect her real estate she formulated an LLC. She now writes off her husband truck since he uses it to take care of the properties. That includes gas, repairs, toll fares, insurance, vehicle registration. It is now paid by the business and is another deduction from her personal expenses. Additionally, she gets to deduct approximately 10% of expenses on mortgage, utilities, furniture, computer, fax and cell phone calls she uses for business. This is more deductions taken away from her personal expenses. The good thing about owning a home-based business is a that you will be able to keep more of the income generated from the business as oppose to giving one-third to Uncle Sam like your job requires.

In summary, Penny is off to a great start. She was able to find the time to do her new business by getting up a little earlier and going to bed a little later. She spends less time doing idle things like watching T.V., reading the newspaper and gossip with her friends and family on the phone. Instead, each time she had a moment, she focused her energies on getting her closer to her financial goal. She stated that even though she is working a little harder, she doesn't feel the impact of it because she is enjoying having control of her financial destiny. She feels more empowered, happy and her self-esteem has improved with each success she has experience. Even her kids have gotten in on the act, they are encouraging her to save because they want to go to a good school. They want their own part-time business because they can see that the power of having their own money will open many wonderful choices.

It hasn't been all roses. She experienced some set backs: She allowed her mother to use her credit card and mom did not pay the bill. It lowered her FICO score. She had to get a new roof on her home just while she was making a big purchase (a house). Someone broke into her car and stole her purse with her credit cards and money. Her response to such tragedies was remarkable. She was doing her wealth conscious work and focus on the positive. She looked for the lesson in each experience and never wavered from accomplishing her goal of becoming a Dynamic Diva Millionaire.

Nina

Final Words

Dynamic Diva Come Out, Come Out Wherever You Are!

Dear Dynamic Divas

Now that you have completed this book you are now being put on notice from the Universe, that it is time not to do "business as usual". You are called to take some action and put to work one, two, three, or all of the ideas in this book to establish yourself on the road to fantastic wealth building.

This is not a time to start making up any excuses as to why today you cannot become financially free. Excuses, like: I am so busy, I do not have the time; or I do not have the right connections; I have already failed before I cannot bear the thought of trying again; are no longer acceptable. You can do anything you put your mind to and you must. The economic climate is not going to change and those who are not prepared will be left behind with a fate of despair and discontent. Please do not be one of those who do not answer the call. The time is now!!!!!!!!!!!!!!!!

In parting words, I want to you to fully understand that I had all the odds against me:

1. I was born into a poor family.

2. I came from a broken home.

3. I was raised by a single mom on welfare.

4. I was black.

5. I was a woman.

6. My dad was a drug dealer

7. I was homeless at a woman shelter with a one year old child when I brought my first house with $36 in my checking account and no job!

But, I understood I was not a product of my circumstances. I believed within my heart that there was a divine force that was so much greater than what was showing up in my life. I knew I had the power to tap into the **Source - The Dynamic Diva inside of me**. The same divine force that resides in me resides in you too. Admit it. There have been times in your life when a spark of inspiration and passion about a particular idea came to you. You got very excited and saw the best outcome. You started to put things in motion. And then, something else happens. Negative thoughts about your abilities came to mind. All the excuse and obstacles came up to tell you, you didn't have the money, time or resources to make it work.

Divas, you will have many peaks and valleys on your wealth journey. They are a necessary means to a better end. Do not let anything that appears as being uncomfortable or difficult have you thinking about giving up on your prosperity dream. These challenges are cleverly disguised as great opportunity to see the best strategy to take in order to accomplish your wealth goal. It is helping you build character, courage, strength, persistence. Additionally, you are learning patients, perseverance and principles you sometimes can not learn any other place. The main reason why it feels so uncomfortable is because you are entering un-chartered territory. You are doing something you have never done before. Remember, how uncomfortable you were when you were first learning how to drive a car or get a college degree. We all have felt nervous and unsure about our abilities when we tried something for the first time. Nevertheless, we made it through those difficult moments, and you will make it through the challenges it takes to become a millionaires-just keep your eye on the prize.

Now, Diva, I implore you now to dust off your dreams. Come on, Dynamic Diva you can do it, there is nothing to it. Bring those fabulous dreams that only you can do to fruition. The ones that no one can do quite the way you can. No one else can sing the songs like you. No one else can play that role in the Broadway show like you can. No one can write the book of all books like you can. No one else can create a multimillion dollar business like you can. You have so much to share and so much to give to the world. That is why you are still here. So, go on Diva do your thang!

I think Nelson Mandela was thinking of you, Diva, when he spoke these most eloquent words at his inaugural speech as President of South Africa:

Our greatest fear is not that we are in adequate. Our greatest fear is that we are powerful beyond measure. It is our light not our darkness that most frightens us. We ask ourselves, "Who am I to be brilliant, gorgeous, talented, and fabulous?"

You are a child of God. Your playing small doesn't serve the world. There's nothing enlightening about shrinking so that other people won't feel insecure around you. You were born to manifest the glory of God that is within you. It's not just in some of us, it's in everyone. And as we let our own light shine, we unconsciously give other people permission to do the same. As we're liberated from our fear, our presence automatically liberates others.

Diva

PAPYRUS PUBLISHING PRODUCT LINE

Check out our fabulous, fun-filled and informative website
www.thedynamicdiva.com/tools.com and
www.thedynamicdiva.com/divatoolsshop.html
for an update of the products we have available for you.

Dynamic Diva Dollars Book

Dynamic Diva Calendar

Dynamic Diva Dollars Prosperity Kit

Dynamic Diva Hats

Dynamic Diva Mugs

Dynamic Diva Shirts

Wealth Chants

MSM Miracles

EXPRESS ORDER FORM

All orders can be expedited on *www.thedynamicdiva.com*

Email orders: *orders@thedynamicdiva.com*

Fax orders: 281.394.3390. *See this form*

Telephone orders: Call 281.394.3384. Have your credit card ready

Postal orders: Papyrus Publishing, Elon Bomani, 5680 Hwy 6 #166, Missouri City, TX. 77459-0000. USA.

Please send the following Books, DVD, CD etc. I understand that I may return any of them for a full refund within 30 days-for any reason, no questions asked.

Please send more free information on:

____Other books, _____ Speaking/Seminars,

____Email/mailing lists,

____Consulting

____Mentor Program

Name: _____

Address: _____

City: _____ State: _____ Zip: _____ - ____

Telephone: _____

Email Address: _____

Sales Tax: Please add 8.25% for products shipped to Texas addresses

Shipping by air: $4 for the first book or CD and $2 for each additional product.

Payment Options: Check   Credit card:

❑ Visa   ❑ MasterCard   ❑ Amex

Card number: _____

Name on Card: _____

Exp. Date_____/ ____ Security Code: _____ (the three digit on the back of the card after card # or the front top digits, on the right side above the credit card # of Amex card)

Please visit us at: *www.thedynamicdiva.com*

Nina

DYNAMIC DIVA DOLLARS
WEALTH WORKSHOP & CERTIFICATION PROGRAM

If the book motivated you, then the Dynamic Diva Dollars Workshop will provide you with the tools to put your wealth goals into action. The first Dynamic Diva Dollars Workshop will cover: developing a Wealth Consciousness, creating a Financial Makeover, build a real estate, stock and business portfolios so you can retire young and rich!

Also, you can become a dynamic diva facilitator/consultant and make money inspiring your sister Divas to become more healthy, wealthy and wise. But first you must be a practitioner of what you will be preaching.

This is a five day intensive hands-on-training workshop in 2008. The seating will be limited so that we can provide an intimate environment and personalized attention to Divas who are really serious about building wealth. So, act now!

Dynamic Diva Dollars Wealth Workshop: $2495.00 per person (For couples, half price for second spouse)

Check *www.thedynamicdiva.com/workshops.html* for more details

Nina

ELECTRONIC MARKETING & SEARCH ENGINE OPTIMIZATION WORKSHOP

This intensive, hands-on-workshop is for the non-technical and technical person who wants to learn how to develop a new career and profit big time as an electronic marketing consultant. Additionally, this is a great class for web designers, web developers and small business owners who want to add a new feature to the services they offer. Moreover, we will teach you how to build a website that is dynamic and make you money. Also, this class will benefit those with a website that aren't drawing any traffic and would like to increase sells. We will teach such interesting topic as how to profit from: teleseminars, webinars, blogging, article writing, copywriting, podcasting and affiliate marketing.

Electronic Marketing Workshop: $2495.00 per person
(For couples, half-price for second spouse)

Check *www.thedynamicdiva.com/workshops.html* for more details

Nina

OTHER EDUCATIONAL MATERIAL, SERVICES AND VALUABLE PRODUCT

BY ELON BOMANI

The Dynamic Diva E-Zine
http://www.thedynamicdiva.com/ezinesubscribe.html

The Dynamic Diva Blog
http://www.thedynamicdiva.com/blog

Internet Marketing Diva Blog
http://internet-marketingdiva.com

Divas Domains- Cheaper Domains than Go-Daddy
http://www.divasdomains.com

Credit Diva- All credit card purchases service
http://www.creditdiva.ecreditdirectory.com

Dynamic Diva Mentor
http://www.thedynamicdiva.com/mentor.html

Dynamic Diva Consultation Packages
http://www.thedynamicdiva.com/consultation.html

Dynamic Diva Lecture and Seminar Information
http://www.thedynamicdiva.com/lecture.html

Dynamic Diva Tools—Books, CDs. DVDs
http://www.thedynamicdiva.com/tools.html

Dynamic Diva Tools-Apparel and other Merchandise
http://www.thedynamicdiva.com/toolsshop.html